To Cynthia
God has great
I pray that thi
you further; I prophesy that
& Purpose, the Dreams & Visions in you
shall manifest in
9ts SEASON!

# Lord Teach Me How to Pray

Enjoy the Journey
Apostle C
2017

*Activating the Keys to the Kingdom to*
*Experience Heaven on Earth!*

*Author - Connie Strickland*

XULON
PRESS

MW00941329

www.xulonpress.com

# *Dedication*

*Father, Son, and Holy Spirit, I give back to you what you have birthed through me.*

*To my mother — from whom I received the mantle to intercede.*

*To all of my family — thank you for your prayers and support!*

*To my children — who keep me on my knees!*

*To the Body of Christ — may you receive an impartation that will shift you from Glory to Glory.*

# *Acknowledgements*

*To all of the Generals of Intercession who have been forerunners for me,*

*To my editor, John Loewen, and proofreaders Cheryl Martin and Gwen Baisley*

*To my personal intercessors, who were "handmaidens" of the Lord,*

*And to all of my spiritual mothers and fathers (you know who you are):*

*Thank you all for assisting me in the "birthing process" and seeing me all the way through delivery!*

# Foreword

**P**rayer and intercession are two of several keys Jesus has given us that provide access into the Kingdom of Heaven. The book you're holding was written by one who's quite familiar with the use of these keys.

From Connie's refreshing explanation of the five attributes of God that motivate us to pray with thanksgiving, to the depths of her exceptional disclosures concerning worship, she's furnished us with a pragmatic, insightful equipping tool.

Connie writes: "God is raising up an army of intercessors who know how to pray strategically and maneuver in many dimensions of intercession. There is a revival that will usher in the rapture of the Church and it will be birthed out by the emerging Kingdom intercessors."

She explains: "There is a new breed of intercessors that God is thrusting forth. They are called Kingdom intercessors. Kingdom intercessors are born again, Spirit filled believers who have accepted the call of God to intercede. Kingdom intercessors are disciplined in prayer, studying the Word of God, and fasting. They live consecrated lives, making themselves available to be a vessel through which God can birth His purposes and plans in the earth realm. Because they have graduated from the School of the Spirit, they know how to maneuver in different dimensions of intercession. They are militant, radical, and know how to engage in spiritual warfare."

She's absolutely on target. Never before has there been such a movement of deeper level prayer throughout the earth. It was at the time of prayer in the temple that John the Baptist's father received an angelic announcement that he would bear a son, who would usher in the first coming of Christ. I'm convinced that we (our generation) have drawn the lot to burn the incense before Christ's second coming. Chapters Five and Six are each worth more than the price of this book! Allow me to give you a peek.

In Chapter Five, Connie explains the "Five Dimensions of Intercession": Strategic Intercession, Prophetic Intercession, Warfare Intercession, Corporate Intercession and Apostolic Intercession.

In Chapter Six, "Overcoming The Belly God", she offers one of the best presentations of the ministry of fasting that I've seen. It's rich; and there are many other wonderful surprises to be discovered here.

Connie's years before the throne and on the front-lines of spiritual warfare uniquely equip her to write this book. But her clear thinking and writing skill are what make it interesting and enjoyable!

Eddie Smith
www.EddieAndAlice.com

# TABLE OF CONTENTS

*Introduction*................................................................*xv*

*Chapter 1* ................................................................*21*
*Understanding the Protocol Necessary*
*to Approach God*

*Chapter 2* ................................................................*47*
*Exposing the Issues of the Heart*

*Chapter 3* ................................................................*72*
*Worship: the Place of Conception*

*Chapter 4* ................................................................*95*
*How to Shift from Prayer to Intercession*

*Chapter 5* ................................................................*115*
*Five Dimensions of Intercession*

*Chapter 6* ................................................................*139*
*Overcoming the "Belly God"*

*Chapter 7* ............................................................*159*
*The Kingdom Language*

*Chapter 8* ............................................................*177*
*Releasing Prophetic Declarations*

# INTRODUCTION

In Luke 11:1, as Jesus was praying in a certain place, one of His disciples approached Him and said, *"...Lord, teach us to pray, as John also taught his disciples."* It was a request that demanded an immediate response. What amazes me is that he did not ask Jesus to teach him how to perform miracles or how to prophesy. What provoked this disciple, who is not identified in the passage, to present this request? It is evident that the disciples had witnessed prayer as a vital part of Jesus life. Jesus led by example. According to the following scripture, Jesus was often found in a place of seclusion, communicating with the Father: *"Very early in the morning, while it was still dark, Jesus got up, left the house and went off to a solitary place, where he prayed"* (Mark 1:35, NIV).

In Luke 18:1, He gives us the command to *"... pray and not give up"* (NIV). The result of Jesus' effective prayer life was a mantle of the supernatural power of God, which flowed in and through His life.

He went forth healing all manner of diseases, casting out demons, and performing miracles. Now let's get back to His disciple's question. Jesus response was to present what we know today as "The Lord's Prayer." This model prayer was an outline that Jesus established for us so that we would know how to approach God. Unfortunately, some believers have made this prayer a ritual, eradicating the very purpose for which Christ intended it. I do not believe that Jesus desired that we memorize the prayer and pray it for the rest of our lives.

As we look throughout the Old and New Testaments, we find Biblical examples of how God used the prayers and intercessions of men and women to transform nations. In this hour, God is calling the Church back to *prayer* so that we can move forward to *intercession.* If we are going to reclaim our nations for God, it is going to take place on our knees. Many intercessors from around the globe are receiving the "burden of the Lord," and the Holy Spirit is teaching us how to pray God's will into the earth.

As you journey through this book, you will discover different kinds of prayer, and learn how all of them are vital in our lives. Each chapter will take you to another dimension, as you learn how to pray from a Kingdom perspective and position. The Bible lets us know that Jesus came to restore the Kingdom. That was His central message. On more than one occasion He said, *"...Repent for the Kingdom of Heaven is at hand" (Matt. 4:17).*

If we are going to experience God's Kingdom in its fullness, we must first learn how to gain entrance into the Kingdom. In Matthew 16:19, Jesus says that He has given us the keys to the Kingdom. What is the purpose of keys? To lock and unlock! In the Bible, keys represent "authority." Prayer and intercession are two of many keys that give us entrance or access into the Kingdom of Heaven.

Simultaneously, we have the authority to close the entrance to the Kingdom of darkness that comes to deter the plans and purposes of God. We accomplish this by utilizing the power of binding and loosing: *"Verily I say unto you, Whatsoever ye shall bind on earth shall be bound in Heaven: and whatsoever ye shall loose on earth shall be loosed in Heaven"* (Matt.18:18).

God desires for you to experience Heaven on earth, and this can be accomplished when you learn how to pray strategically. Prayer and intercession are the most needed ministries in the Church; however they have become the most neglected. Sure, there are Churches that religiously have their "once a week prayer" and early morning prayer on Sundays. However, the ministry of prayer and intercession is absent in many of our Churches. The following manifestations reveal this truth:

- It is evident that prayer is absent in our Churches when Sunday after Sunday the altar is filled with believers. God told us to pray for the harvest, and to pray that laborers would go out into the vineyard. Jesus said that he did not come to call the righteous but sinners to repentance. Our altars need to be filled with those who need salvation!

- It is evident that prayer is absent in our Churches when worship lasts only five minutes. As a result of the spirit of religion running rampant in the Church, time becomes a factor as it relates to worship. Worship in some Churches has become part of the program. But according to John 4:24, God is seeking true worshippers, those that would worship Him in spirit and truth and are not bound by time and circumstance.

- It is evident that prayer is absent in our Churches when demons manifest. This manifestation distracts the Body of Christ, which sees it as a move of God, because the gift of discerning of spirits is not flowing. Demons have been assigned to Churches and ministries. Their assignment is to come in and deter the plan of God for that region. A church that has a ministry of prayer and is equipped with trained and skilled intercessors is able to recognize the strategies of the enemy and expose these demonic spirits. When strategic prayer is going forth, God gives you insight into every assignment of the enemy. Intercessors not only pray, but they watch as well. In this hour, apostolic ministries are mobilizing intercessors, watchmen, and gate-keepers in the Church so that they can be effective in advancing the Kingdom.

- Prayer is also absent in our Churches when we see constant warfare between leaders and their congregations. The spirit of jealousy, competition, and division also run rampant in the Church. They are all manifestations of the flesh. Prayer brings our flesh under subjection. When our flesh is under subjection, we will be able to come together in unity as we advance the Kingdom of God.

Yes, these are real manifestations in our churches as a result of prayer being absent! As you journey through each chapter of this book, my prayer is that God will speak to you, and that you will shift to the next dimension in prayer and intercession. *I decree that you are moving from a place of complacency, and that God is stretching you and thrusting you into new realms of His presence and revelation. I decree that your prayer life will never be the same!*

*~ God has established a protocol necessary to approach Him. We cannot approach Him the way we approach one another. He extends the invitation for us to come into His presence by the order that He established in Psalm 100. ~*

## Chapter 1

# UNDERSTANDING THE PROTOCOL NECESSARY TO APPROACH GOD

When President Obama and the First Lady went to England to meet the Queen, they were briefed so that they could understand the "Royal Protocol." It was clear that they could not approach the Queen in the same manner that they approached other dignitaries. It was reported that the First Lady touched the Queen as they gathered to take a picture. The protocol states that you do not touch the Queen unless she invites you to do so. Therefore, the First Lady broke protocol!

To break protocol is a sign of disrespect, although the First Lady meant no disrespect. This inadvertently occurred when she touched the Queen. My friend, royalty demands that we follow the protocol established by kings, queens, prime ministers, and other dignitaries.

As citizens of the Kingdom, God has also established a protocol for His people through which we approach Him. The Bible declares that the only way to the Father is through Jesus (Yeshua). He is King of Kings, and Lord of Lords! Therefore, we cannot be passive in the way that we approach Him. God gives us a directive on how to approach Him, which is revealed in Psalm 100:

- **Make** *a joyful noise unto the Lord, all ye lands,*

- **Serve** *the Lord with gladness;* **Come** *before his presence with singing*

- **Know** *ye that the Lord he is God: it is he that hath made us, and not we ourselves; we are his people, and the sheep of his pasture*

- **Enter** *into his gates with thanksgiving, and into his courts with praise, be thankful unto him, and bless his name. For the Lord is good; His mercy is everlasting and His truth endureth to all generations.*

As we examine this passage of Scripture, we will observe that the first word in each sentence begins with a verb. We know that verbs are usually action words, requiring us to do something. Each of these verbs reveals an expression of what our attitude should be or what we should do as we enter into the presence of God:

1. **Make:** This means to formulate, or form. Words must be formed into noise, which must come out of your mouth. It must be more than just "air," but words that are communicated. You cannot make a joyful noise with your mouth closed!

2. **Serve:** The Hebrew connotation is "to enslave." A submitted slave desires to please his master. Our countenance should reflect the joy of the Lord as we enter the house of God to unite with other believers.

3. **Come:** The Hebrew connotation means "to go, or abide." As we move into His presence with songs of joy, we usher in the Heavenly host to join us on earth. This union produces an atmosphere for the Spirit of the Lord to move in an unprecedented way.

4. **Know:** The Hebrew word for know is "yada," which means "to be acquainted with." God desires that we not just know of Him, but that we have an intimate relationship with Him.

5. **Enter:** This implies to "come in." This invitation is not from the praise and worship leader, but from God. It is personal. He invites us and yearns for us to come into His presence. Because we know Him, we come with the cry of "Abba Father," which is interpreted "Daddy God" in "Connie's Concordance."

I hope that you have a clear perception of the protocol necessary to approach God. If we miss verses one and two of Psalm 100, then we've missed the protocol. God has always provided a pattern on how mankind is to approach Him.

In the Old Testament He used the Tabernacle of Moses as a pattern for the children of Israel to enter into His presence. Through the New Covenant, we have become that temple where the Spirit of the Lord dwells (I Corinthians 3:16).

### *The Weapon of Praise*

Praise is a type of prayer where we express our love to God for who He is. The word "praise" literally means to *"commend, to applaud, or magnify."* God commands us to praise Him. It is not an option. Psalms 150:6 says, *"Let everything that hath breath praise the Lord."* The Bible identifies seven Hebrew words for *"praise":*

- **Halal** – "to boast; or celebrate" (Psalms 150:1).

- **Yadah** – "to lift or extend the hand" (Psalms 63:1).
- **Towdah** – "an expression of thanks" (Psalms 42:4).
- **Shabach** - "to shout or address in a loud tone" (Psalms 47:1).
- **Barak** - "to kneel down" - an act of adoration (Psalms 34:1).
- **Zamar** - "to play music" (Psalms 138:1).
- **Tehillah** - "to sing hymns" (Psalms 23:1).

All of these manifestations of praise emanate out of a heart that loves and fears God, and acknowledges that He is worthy to be praised! When we praise God, we release His supernatural power to bring us victory in every area of our lives. Praise is also a weapon of warfare against the enemy. Satan wants your praise, and the only way he can get it is if you do not open your mouth.

When we release our praise in the atmosphere, it confuses the enemy. The Bible declares that the devil comes to kill, steal, and destroy. The devil knows that if he can keep you from praising God, he can hold you captive. He understands the power of praise. We must not forget that he was an anointed cherub in Heaven. He was the praise and worship leader. However, pride consumed him, and he was kicked out of Heaven with a third of the angels.

Do you know what happens when you do not praise your God? Your circumstances begin to appear bigger than your God. When we began to focus on our problems and circumstances, we give place to the devil. The Word of God tells us to give no place to the devil. Jesus told us that in this world we would have tribulation, but to be of good cheer, because He overcame the world (John 16:33). That's good news! Therefore, if Jesus overcame the world and He is in us, we too can overcome the world!

We are commanded to cast our cares upon the Lord, because He cares for us. If we do not apply this Scripture to our lives, we open the door for the spirit of heaviness. The spirit of heaviness is a "root" spirit (strongman) that manifests the following fruits:

- depression
- oppression
- despair
- hopelessness
- rejection
- discouragement
- shame
- self-pity

Many believers go to Church every Sunday with these fruits evident in their lives, and leave the same way they came. Are any of these fruits evident in your life? If so, it is time to close the door today. God said that He would give you a garment of praise for the spirit of heaviness (Isaiah 61:3).

When you began to praise God, your focus shifts from your ***problems*** to His ***promises.*** This is the place where you began to make prophetic declarations of the promises of God over your life. A prophetic declaration is when you decree the Word of God over your situation. The Word of God says that we can decree a thing and it shall be established (Job 22:28).

There are promises available in God's Word that you can apply to every problem in your life. However, some of the promises are conditional. Many believers live defeated lives because they do not meet the conditions necessary to receive the promise, or they do not know what promises are available to them because they do not know the Word of God. God declares in His Word *"my people are destroyed from lack of knowledge"* (Hosea 4:6, NIV).

### *God Dwells In The Midst Of Praise*

I am reminded of how the mothers of the Church would always encourage me to praise God when I was going through hard times. They would say something like, *"praise Him in spite of."* Well, for a baby Christian that is easier said than done. It was the following scripture that gave me the encouragement to breakthrough my circumstances: *"But thou are holy, O thou that inhabitest the praises of Israel."* (Psalms 22:3).

The word "inhabitest" in its Hebrew connotation means *"to dwell."* I know that we have traditionally confessed, "When the praises go up the Blessings come down." However, I announce to you today that, "When the praises go up, God comes down." I had to realize that having a "pity party" was not going to move God. God dwells in the atmosphere of praise. When God shows up your enemy will flee! Let's hear the testimony of Jehoshaphat who understood the power of praise:

> *And Jehoshaphat bowed his head with his face to the ground: and all Judah and the inhabitants of Jerusalem fell before the Lord, worshipping the Lord. And the Levites, of the children of the Kohathites, and of the children of the Korhites, stood up to praise the Lord God of Isarel with a loud voice on high.*

> *And they rose up early in the morning, and went forth into the wilderness of Tekoa: and as they went forth, Jehoshaphat stood and said, Hear me, O Judah and ye inhabitants of Jerusalem; Believe in the Lord your God, so shall ye be established; believe his prophets, so shall ye prosper. And when he had consulted with the people, he appointed singers unto the Lord and that should praise the beauty of holiness, as they went out before the army, and to say, Praise the Lord; for his mercy endureth for ever. And when they began to sing and to praise, the Lord set ambushments against the children of Ammon and Moab, and Mount Seir, which were*

*come against Judah; and they were smitten*
(2 Chronicles 20:18-22).

This passage of Scripture reveals what happens
when we release praise:

a.  Praise changes the atmosphere
b.  Praise thwarts the plans of your enemies
c.  Praise builds up your inner man

I encourage you to **take a praise break now!**
There is a praise down on the inside of you that the
enemy cannot steal. It is called **"His Praise."** David
declared it in Psalms 34:1: "*I will bless the Lord at all
times: his Praise shall continually be in my mouth.*"

> *I prophesy now that you will begin to release*
> *"His Praise." I bind the spirit of heavi-*
> *ness and I command you in the Name of*
> *Jesus to loose the reader now! Your power*
> *is destroyed In Jesus Name! I loose the*
> *garment of praise upon the reader now and I*
> *decree and declare that the yoke is destroyed*
> *because of the anointing flowing from this*
> *prayer in Jesus Name. I declare that they are*
> *being elevated above their circumstances, in*
> *Jesus Name!*

### *The Gates of Thanksgiving*

Thanksgiving is another type of prayer where
we express our gratitude toward God's *faithful-*

*ness, kindness, goodness, grace and mercy.* If God decided not to bless us again, He has done more than enough for us. Yet, many continue to murmur and complain about what they don't have, instead of being grateful for what they do have. Paul exhorts us in 1 Thessalonians 5:18 to give thanks in everything. Why? *"Because this is God's will for us in Christ Jesus."*

In layman's terms, God is not glorified when we shift into the complaining and murmuring mode. If you want to bring Him glory, let the fruit of your lips be filled with praise and thanksgiving. No matter what you are going through right now, the Word says that *"...all things work together for good to those who love God and who are called according to His purpose..."* (Romans 8:28).

When we give thanks unto the Lord, we convey to Him that we appreciate everything that He has done for us. Oftentimes, our circumstances will contradict what God has promised but, our response should be, "God is in control." When we take this stance we acknowledge God's sovereignty. God is the supreme ruler and as the song states, "He has the whole world in His hands."

Let's look more closely at the attributes of God that motivate us to give thanks to Him:

## 1.  The Faithfulness of God

Faithfulness is defined as *"dependability, loyalty, and stability."* Lamentations 3:23 declares that the "faithfulness" of God is great, implying that we can depend on God! It indicates that God is reliable and trustworthy. He keeps His covenant with mankind. The question is can God depend on us?

According to Psalms 35:6, God's faithfulness is infinite. It surpasses our understanding. However, it is an attribute that God has ascribed to the believer, and is one of the fruit of the Spirit (Galatians 5:22). As believers, we should strive to be faithful in all that we do for the Lord and one another. The Bible declares that if we are faithful over a few things, God will make us ruler over much.

Our faithfulness need to be demonstrated in our daily lives. We need to be faithful on our jobs, in our churches, and in our relationships. Has God given you an assignment in your church? If so, you should be faithful in completing that assignment. All that you do in completing the assignment should be unto the glory of the Lord.

If you are not working in your Church, why are you there? God does not lead us to a ministry to occupy the seats. When God lead us to a church it is because He wants to use us in that ministry. Yes, we do understand that we must go through the Church protocol of attending the different training classes to equip us to do the work of the ministry. Upon completion of the training we should be ready to serve in the area of ministry where we believe God is calling us to serve. However, many believers remain in a place of complacency because of a spirit of fear and rebellion. These spirits deter us from moving forward in the things of God.

The Word declares that the faithful man shall abound in blessings. Our desire should be to one day stand before **JESUS** and hear Him say, *"Well done thou good and faithful servant..."*

## 2.  The Kindness of God

Nelson's Bible dictionary describes kindness as, *"God's loyal love and favor toward His people."* According to Psalms 117:2, God's kindness is great towards His people: *"For his merciful kindness is great toward us: and the truth of the LORD endureth for ever..."*

It is essential to note that the kindness of God was demonstrated through His love for mankind by giving up His only Son: *"For God so loved the world, that he gave his only begotten Son, that whosoever believeth in him should not perish, but have everlasting life."* (John 3:16).

God's kindness was evident when, in spite of our sinful nature, He sent His only Son to take our place on the Cross: *"For He hath made him to be sin for us, who knew no sin; that we might be made the righteousness of God in him" (2* Corinthians 5:21).

It was this kindness that afforded us the opportunity to be reconciled back to Him. We are no longer strangers but are fellow citizens in the Kingdom (Hebrews 2:19). The word "kindness" also denotes compassion. I heard someone once say that compassion is more powerful than anger. As believers we should be experiencing this truth. It was the compassion of God that caused Him to promise that He would not destroy the earth again with water. It was the compassion of Christ that prompted Him to ask God to forgive those who crucified Him. Essentially, when you are driven by compassion it will cause you to meet a need. God saw that mankind was in need of a Savior, so He sent a Redeemer, in the person of His Son.

As believers, this attribute should be part of our everyday lives if we are going to reach the lost. We must learn to look beyond the sin in their lives, and look into the wilderness of their hearts. God hates homosexuality but not the homosexual. As believers we must love what God loves, and hate what God hates. The Word says that *"…he who win souls is wise."* (Proverbs 11:30, NIV).

If we are going to be effective witnesses we must mature in the Spirit so that the fruit of kindness can manifest in our lives. Remember the lyrics *"What the World needs now is love sweet Love"*? Well, I would like to change the lyrics to declare *"What the world needs now, is Love, Agape Love, and it only comes, from our Father Above"*!

This Agape Love will cause us to extend kindness to those around us. As we observe the condition of our world, we can truly attest that if more kindness was exemplified, homeless, hunger, and violence would be a thing of the past. I know that we have heard it said that "we live in a dog eat dog world," and "every man for himself," but let a disaster strike and see what happens!

We got an opportunity to witness mankind come together as kindness was demonstrated during the 9/11 terrorist attack, the tsunami which occurred right after Christmas in 2004, Hurricane Katrina, and Hurricane Rita. It is so unfortunate that disaster has to strike before we can exhibit kindness to our fellow man. However, God just needs one person who is willing to make the difference. Are you that person? Let God be glorified through you today as you show kindness to your fellow man.

## 3. The Goodness of God

As a child I can remember going to Church and hearing the pastor say, "God is good all the time," and the congregation would respond and say, "And all the time God is good." We continue to hear this even in our Churches today. However, we need to have a clear perception of the goodness of God. Our perception of the goodness of God should not be predicated on a theological or religious fact. The goodness of God should be evident in our daily lives. The Word declares that, *"...goodness and love will follow me all the days of my life, and I will dwell in the house of the LORD forever"* (Psalms 23:6, NIV).

Goodness is defined as *"the quality of being good; praiseworthy character; moral excellence."* According to Psalms 34:8, God is good: *"O taste and see that the LORD is good: blessed is the man that trusteth in him."*

While Christians and sinners both believe that God is good, His goodness is particularly manifested in the lives of those who trust in Him.

Oftentimes when I am witnessing to unbelievers and bring up the truth about hell, they respond with an outburst like, "God is too good to send people to hell." My immediate response to them would be, "You are correct. God is not sending anyone to hell."

God does not want mankind to perish. According to John 3:16, God's goodness is bestowed on each and every sinner by giving them provision for their sins through Jesus Christ. Out of His goodness He gives mankind a choice to either accept or reject His Son!

It is the choice we make that determines where we will spend eternity. It is the goodness of God that draws us to repentance (Romans 2:4). Let us observe the exhortation from the Psalmist in Psalms 107:8-9: *"Oh that men would praise the LORD for his goodness, and for his wonderful works to the children of men! For he satisfieth the longing soul, and filleth the hungry soul with goodness."*

I am reminded of a church that I attended when I lived in California many years ago. It was a Church of God In Christ. On Sunday evenings after praise and worship, we would have what they call "Testimony Service." Every Testimony Service, you can count on some Church mother, or aspiring missionary to stand up and exhort the people of God through the song *God is a Good God.* As we praised God through this song, the Church would go up to another level. People would be running around the Church and dancing before the Lord.

I realized that I was in the midst of a people who experienced the goodness of God, and appreciated it. I want you to know that I was not just sitting there observing. I was a participant because, *"When I think of the goodness of Jesus and all that He is has done for me, my soul cries out HALLELUJAH! Thank God for saving me!"*

### 4. The Grace of God

The word "grace" is defined as *"Favor or kindness shown without regard to the worth or merit of the one who receives it, and in spite of what that person deserves."* Grace and mercy are the key attributes of God. Throughout Bible history and in our own lives we can attest to the grace of God. We know that in the beginning when God made man, He made man for fellowship. However, there was a time in Scripture where God was so grieved by the conduct of man that He literally hated that He had created man. Genesis 6: 6-7 reveals this truth:

> *And it repented the LORD that he had made man on the earth, and it grieved him at his heart. And the LORD said, I will destroy man whom I have created from the face of the earth; both man, and beast, and the creeping thing, and the fowls of the air; for it repenteth me that I have made them.*

In the midst of wickedness and corruption, there was one man found just and perfect in his generation. For the Bible declares that Noah walked with God, and found grace in the eyes of God. When God destroyed the earth with the flood, Noah and his family were saved. God used Noah to birth His purposes and plans in the earth. Noah obeyed God and as a result is noted as one of the heroes of faith, according to Hebrews 11:7.

The grace of God was upon Noah to complete the assignment God gave Him. When we walk in obedience to God's will, His grace will be extended to us. Not only will we have favor with God, but with man also. The following Scripture reveals the truth: *Let not mercy and truth forsake thee: bind them about thy neck; write them upon the table of thine heart: So shalt thou find favour and good understanding in the sight of God and man* (Proverbs 3:3,4).

Praise God for His Amazing Grace! It is far beyond our comprehension. No matter what we are faced with today, God's grace (unmerited favor) is available to us. The Bible declares that His grace is sufficient to us.

### 5. The Mercy of God

As believers we should appreciate the mercy of God. Why? Because He did not give us what we deserved. As we focus on this word we need to understand that mercy is the inverse of grace:

- Mercy is "not getting what you do deserve," or "*withheld punishment.*"

- Grace is "getting what you don't deserve," or "*unmerited favor.*"

Our finite mind could never truly, understand the mercy of God. I have often heard people testify of God being a God of a second chance. This is not a true statement. If God only gave second chances, you and I would not be here today. He is a God of another chance. He continues to give us chance after chance, and it never ends. Why? Because God's mercy is eternal and unchanging! It is from "...*everlasting to everlasting*" (Psalms 103:17). We also see that, "*It is because of the LORD's mercies that we are not consumed, because his compassions fail not. They are new every morning: great is thy faithfulness*" (Lamentations 3:23).

It was God's mercy that brought the children of Israel out of bondage to Egypt. In spite of their perpetual rebellion against Him, God's love for His people averted His judgment and mercy was extended again, and again, and again. It was God's mercy and love that quickened us when we were dead in our sins: "*But God, who is rich in mercy, for his great love wherewith he loved us, Even when we were dead in sins, hath quickened us together with Christ, (by grace ye are saved;)*" (Ephesians 2:4-5).

Although God is a merciful God, He will not allow sin to go unpunished. As we have seen in our own society, God's judgment has been poured out on the earth. The Word declares that judgment will begin in the household of God. We must not take God's mercy for granted. As He extends it to us, we need to extend it to our fellow man.

Jesus taught us in the beatitudes that "*Blessed are the merciful for they shall obtain mercy*" (Matt. 5:7). As we demonstrate God's mercy to others, we will receive more mercy from God.

### *An Attitude of Gratitude*

Throughout my life's journey, my past experiences, whether good or bad, have taught me how to maintain an attitude of gratitude. I realize that I am who I am today because of God, and everything that I have is because of God. It is in Him that I live, move and have my being. This mentality will certainly keep you in a spirit of humility and close the door to the spirit of pride.

We must never forget where God has brought us from. God delivered many of us out of a "horrible pit." Yes, we were on our way to hell and the power of God snatched us out of the hands of the enemy! Somebody was praying for us. The Bible declares that the prayers of the righteous avail much! Today we are recipients of those manifested prayers, and now fulfilling our destiny and purpose.

In Luke 17:12-19, we find a true expression of gratitude from a man who, before his touch from Jesus, was isolated, afflicted, and left in a state of hopelessness. Many have preached this familiar text, however, the revelation that God revealed to me through this text gave me a new outlook on the meaning of gratitude. Let's review this passage of Scripture and allow the Lord to speak to you:

> *12 And as he entered into a certain village, there met him ten men that were lepers, which stood afar off:*

*13 And they lifted up their voices, and said, Jesus, Master, have mercy on us.*

*14 And when he saw them, he said unto them, Go shew yourselves unto the priests. And it came to pass, that, as they went, they were cleansed.*

*15 And 1 of them, when he saw that he was healed, turned back, and with a loud voice glorified God,*

*16 And fell down on his face at his feet, giving him thanks: and he was a Samaritan.*

*17 And Jesus answering said, Were there not ten cleansed? but where are the nine?*

*18 There are not found that returned to give glory to God, save this stranger.*

*19 And he said unto him, Arise, go thy way: thy faith hath made thee whole.*

Here we see an account of Jesus entering into a certain village between Samaria and Galilee. In that village were ten lepers who were afflicted with leprosy from birth. Leprosy is a chronic, infectious disease characterized by sores, scabs, and white shining spots beneath the skin. Old Testament Law was quite detailed in its instructions regarding recognition and quarantine of those with leprosy. Any contact with lepers defiled the persons who touched them.

Can you imagine how these ten lepers must have felt being isolated from society? They had no individual identities because they were identified as lepers. We know that identity is imperative in our society because it describes your individuality. This truth is evident, as we are required to produce certain documents at birth, such as a birth certificate and a social security card. As we progress in life there are other required documents that our state demands that we have. Without an established identity you are left wondering who you are and where you fit it in.

The good news is that even though leprosy was considered incurable, we see the miraculous power of God healing many people of leprosy in both the Old and New Testaments. God struck Miriam with leprosy and then declared that she would be healed in seven days (Numbers 12).

Jesus gives this mandate to his disciples: *"Heal the sick, cleanse the lepers, raise the dead, cast out devils: freely ye have received, freely give"* (Matthew 10:8).

I want you to perceive the severity of this disease, and how one individual was truly grateful to be healed of it. The text reveals that Jesus healed ten lepers, however, only one came back to say thank you! This is an expression of gratitude in action. Yes, these simple words *"thank you"* were expressed as this Samaritan fell down at the feet of a Jew and began glorifying God.

There is more revelation to this passage of Scripture that we need to grasp. It was not typical in those days for Samaritans and Jews to interact among each other. In fact, they literally hated each other. There is a lot of history behind this truth that we will not disclose today, however, the point I want you to see is that this man was determined to press beyond tradition and religion to receive his healing. Because he came back and glorified God, he was not only healed physically, but spiritually as well. Therefore, he received a blessing that the other nine did not receive. Jesus told him that his faith had made him whole (Matthew 10:19).

The word "whole" in the Greek means *"to save or deliver."* As a result of him releasing his faith, the leper received deliverance through the healing power of Jesus. Now he had an identity. He was no longer identified as a leper or stranger, but as a fellow citizen in the Kingdom of God.

What was the attitude of the other nine lepers? Well, it is quite clear they felt like Jesus was obligated to heal them. I am sure that they heard about the ministry of Jesus, and the miraculous signs that were following Him. However, their attitude was, *"I got what I wanted. I've no need to stick around."* Jesus even inquired about the other nine lepers' whereabouts when only one came back (verse 17).

The nine lepers demonstrated an attitude of "ungratefulness." To be ungrateful is a sin. This type of attitude implies that you do not appreciate what God has done for you. Unfortunately, many believers are just like the nine lepers, as they take the blessings of God for granted. Just like the nine lepers they feel that God is obligated to bless them.

What we fail to realize is that God is only obligated to bless us as we walk in obedience to His will. We must cease from complaining and murmuring about what we don't have, and be thankful for that which we do have. Let us not forget the blessings that have been bestowed on us that we did not even ask for. God blessed us just because He wanted to.

We can truly learn from the nine lepers in this story. The challenge is to be grateful for all God has done for us. We should not begin our day without acknowledging God. He who never sleeps nor slumbers (Psalm 121:4), watches over us in a world of chaos. When we receive our morning touch from him, and before our feet hit the floor, we need to tell Him "thank you."

When I look around me and see people that are blind and not complaining, I appreciate the eyes that God has given me. When I am driving to work and look on the other side of the freeway and see a car accident, I not only pray for those in the accident, but thank God for His angels watching over me.

We must not take the life that God has afforded us for granted. The Word declares that *"Blessed is the nation whose God is the Lord"* (Psalm 32:12)! In America we have been afforded the privilege to express our beliefs beyond the Church doors. We can pray on the street corners and not be arrested. We can give God praise and not be martyred. This is a blessing because there are many other nations that do not have this privilege. Every day we should be cognizant of the blessings that God has bestowed on us and take the time to tell Him **"THANK YOU!"**

### *Application: A Prayer of Praise and Thanksgiving*

*Father, I bless your name today. I acknowledge that you are God and that there is none like you in all the earth. You are the only true and living God. Great is your name and greatly to be praised. O Lord my God how excellent is your name in all the earth! I Bless you Father, Glory and Honor belongs to you O' Lord. You are the Almighty God, and Worthy to be Praised! Hallelujah to the King of Kings and the Lord of Lords! How I bless your name today O Lord. You are an awesome God! How I praise your name today! I lift you up! Glory! Glory! Glory!*

*Thank you Father for blessing me to be in the land of the living! Thank you for watching over me and my family last night. Thank you for your angels whom you have given charge over me. I acknowledge that this is the day that the Lord has made and I choose to rejoice and be glad in it. Thank you Father for your mercy that is new in my life today. Thank you that goodness and mercy will follow me all the days of my life.*

*Thank you for Your grace that is sufficient to me. Thank you Lord that all of my needs are met today according to your riches and Glory! Thank you for divine health and strength. Thank you for Your peace in the midst of the storms. Thank you for joy - unspeakable joy! Thank you Lord that my life is hid in You. Thank you Lord for another opportunity to serve You and my fellow man* **(Continue to praise God by clapping your hands and telling Him Thank you).**

*~ Many believers experience unanswered prayers because of "Heart Failure." A pure heart is a prerequisite for answered prayer.*

*~*

## Chapter 2

# EXPOSING THE ISSUES OF THE HEART

In Jeremiah 33:1 believers find the assurance that their prayers are not only being heard, but answered. God delights in answering the prayers of His children. He instructs us to call upon Him. As we do, He promises to answer us! However, we need to examine the condition of our heart. It will determine whether our prayers are answered or not! Psalms 66:18 says, *"If I regard iniquity in my heart, the Lord will not hear me."*

What is iniquity? Webster describes iniquity as *"the absence of moral or spiritual value."* We can attest that iniquity is prevalent in our society today, as we observe a decline in moral and spiritual values. Jesus used three words to describe the generation of this age: wicked, perverse, and adulterous.

However, in the midst of this generation lies a remnant. Paul describes this remnant in 1 Peter 2:9: *"But you are a chosen people, a royal priesthood, a holy nation, a people belonging to God, that you may declare the praises of him who called you out of darkness into his wonderful light."*

According to this Scripture, believers are the chosen people that God called out of darkness into His marvelous light! The Word declares that we are the light of the world (Matthew 5:14). However, if our light is supposed to represent God's glory, our hearts must be pure.

It is clear from Psalms 66:18 that if our hearts are full of iniquity, God will not hear us. And if God doesn't hear us, we might as well be talking to the man on the moon - our prayers will go unanswered. That's why we must on a daily basis acknowledge our sins before the Lord. The Word declares that there is nothing hidden that shall not be revealed. This is called exposure!

To expose means to uncover or reveal the identity of someone, or something. When God exposes the intents and motives of our heart, it is for the purpose of transformation in the inner man. The Bible declares that God searches the heart of man and He knows what's in our hearts. Jeremiah 17: 9-10 says, *"The heart is deceitful above all things, and desperately wicked: who can know it? I the LORD search the heart, I try the reins, even to give every man according to his ways, and according to the fruit of his doings."*

The word "heart" in this text does not refer to the organ which pumps blood. Rather, when looking at the original Hebrew context, it implies that place where our will, intellect, and emotions are stored. It is that which we think, trust, understand, obey, rebel, and which becomes bitter, offended, angry, cheerful, and proud. In other words, the heart is not just the emotional aspect of man; it is the whole of his inner self, the seat of our personality.

We are instructed in Proverbs 23:4 to keep our heart with all diligence; for out of it are the issues of life. The word "keep" in this verse means *"to guard or watch."* It is important to note that we must guard our heart from any/and all manifestation of the fruit of the flesh. The Word says that what is in our heart is revealed through what we say (Matthew 12:34). So in laymen terms, whatever is in your heart will eventually come to light. It is just waiting for the opportune time.

In the natural realm "heart failure" means that the heart's pumping power is weaker than normal. The blood moves through the heart and body at a slower rate, and pressure in the heart increases. Therefore, the heart cannot pump enough oxygen and nutrients to meet the body's needs. Heart failure is a serious condition. About five million people in the United States have heart failure, and the number is growing every day. It contributes to or causes about 300,000 deaths each year. Heart failure does not mean that your heart has stopped or is about to stop working. It means that your heart is not able to pump blood the way that it should. If our body is going to get the oxygen and nutrients needed to function properly, we must have a healthy heart.

Now let's relate heart failure to the spiritual dimension. We will identify heart failure as unresolved issues that lay dormant in our inner man that deter our spiritual growth and maturity. In order for us to reach the maturity level that God is calling us to, we must have a pure heart. Unfortunately, many believers walk in bondage because of "heart failure." As a result of unresolved issues in their hearts, they are not moving towards their destiny and purpose.

When we exhibit a pure heart, we will produce the fruit of the Spirit as described in Galatians 5:22-23: *"But the fruit of the Spirit is love, joy, peace, longsuffering, gentleness, goodness, faith, meekness, temperance: against such there is no law."* We were chosen to bear fruit, and when the fruit of the Spirit is evident in our lives, God is glorified!

I ask the Lord on a daily basis to examine my heart and show me the areas where I need deliverance. I know how imperative it is as an intercessor to pray out of a pure heart. In Psalm 24:3, the writer asks, *"Who shall ascend into the hill of the LORD? or who shall stand in his holy place?"* He then answers the question in the next verse: *"He that hath cleans hands and a pure heart; who hath not lifted up his soul unto vanity, nor sworn deceitfully"* (Psalms 24:4). God will not receive prayers that are not offered out of a pure heart!

A pure heart produces pure motives. In this hour God is judging the motives and intents of our heart. God has revealed to me that many are doing great things in His name, but their motives are not pure. As a result of impure motives, many leaders are being exposed. Unfortunately, the exposure has caused some to lose their ministries and churches. We must be like David and ask God to *"Create in me a clean heart, O God; and renew a right spirit within me"* (Psalm 51:10).

### *The Cause of Heart Failure*

What is the cause of heart failure in the life of the believer? As I stated earlier, unresolved issues are the contributing factor to heart failure. When we fail to resolve these issues, they become personal strongholds that hold us captive. Paul gives us three directives in 2 Corinthians 10:4-5 on how we are to overcome these strongholds:

> *For the weapons of our warfare are not carnal, but mighty through God to the pulling down of strongholds; Casting down imaginations, and every high thing that exalteth itself against the knowledge of God, and bringing*

*into captivity every thought to the obedience of Christ.*

Let's define the word "stronghold" in this text. A stronghold has to do with the way we think. Webster define stronghold as *"a fortified place or fortress."* Our mind is the place where the enemy sets up fortress. Therefore, the battlefield is in the mind. I was blessed by Joyce Meyer's book *The Battlefield of the Mind* many years ago. I learned through this book how to meditate and think on the Word of God. The way we think, whether good or bad, influences our behavior.

When wrong thinking is believed and acted upon as if it is the truth, it becomes a stronghold in a person's life from which the enemy controls them. In her book, *Possessing the Gates of the Enemy,* Cindy Jacobs identifies several types of strongholds. For the purpose of this chapter, we will focus on "personal strongholds." The Lord revealed to me that many believers have opened doors for the enemy (given the enemy a legal right to come in), and as a result, they are being held captive. If we are going to walk in victory in every area of our lives, we must identify these personal strongholds.

God is calling the church to maturity. God desires for us to mature into that spiritual house referred to in 1 Peter 2:5, so that we can maximize our full potential. I want to identify three personal strongholds that held me captive for many years that may be evident in your life. As I confronted them, God delivered me and set me free. I pray that the Holy Spirit will speak to you through this insight and give you the strength to confront these and any other strongholds in your life.

## *Identifying Personal Strongholds*

### 1. The Stronghold of *Unforgiveness*

Unforgiveness in the heart of the believer is like cancer in the organs of one's body. Like cancer, it spreads throughout the body, causing the believer to be in a state of perpetual bondage. When we harbor unforgiveness in our hearts, we open a portal for the enemy. Jesus came to set the captives free. The Bible instructs us to give no place to the devil. (Ephesians 4:27). Forgiveness is not an option, it is a command. God has given us the power to forgive. He leaves the choice of whether we do or not up to us. In Matthew 6:14-15, Jesus gives us this directive on forgiveness: *"For if ye forgive men their trespasses, your heavenly Father will also forgive you: But if ye forgive not men their trespasses, neither will your Father forgive your trespasses."*

When forgiveness is authentic, the power of God is released to heal us emotionally. God spoke to me many years ago and told me how imperative it was for me to forgive everyone who had hurt me. The Lord revealed this to me when I was at a conference hosted by one of my spiritual mothers. It was through this ministry, that God revealed to me the power of forgiveness.

The Lord spoke to me and told me that I needed to forgive my biological father for abandoning me. I was 38 years old when I attended this conference, and I did not even realize that I was harboring unforgiveness against my father. It was an issue that was rooted down on the inside, which apparently I had suppressed for years. However, the Lord exposed it, and I had to confront this issue before I could move to the next level in God. All I remember about my father was that he was a liar. He told me that he would do things that he never did. Nevertheless, I had to be honest with God and release the pain that was associated with abandonment.

It was like the Lord took me back in time and showed me how much of my personality was formed as a result of this act from my father. As a child, I was very rebellious, and by the time I was seventeen, I was involved in drugs and sexual promiscuity. I praise God that my mother had planted the Word of God in me. The Bible declares that one plants, one waters, but God grants the increase (I Corinthians 3:6). By God's grace, the prayers of my mother and many other godly influences in my life prevailed over the purposes and plans of the enemy. At the age of 29, I totally surrendered my life to the Lord.

During this conference the Lord gave me the grace and strength to forgive my father. The enemy could no longer torment me regarding this issue because the power of God delivered me from my past. As a result of this liberty, I am able to minister to other men and women who need deliverance in this area. Jesus became the Father I never knew, and Daddy God has filled that void in my life. He has also blessed me with spiritual fathers whom He has used to impart into my life.

Now, the objective of this testimony is to get you, the reader, to understand that forgiveness is essential to your spiritual development, growth, and maturity. I have ministered to many believers who struggle with unforgiveness. They are deceived to think that they can skip over unforgiveness. Beloved, you cannot skip over unforgiveness! To harbor unforgiveness in your heart is a *sin.*

When you choose not to forgive, you open doors for many other spirits. Yes, it is a fact that most of us were victims of situations in our past that may have traumatized us, however, no matter what we have experienced, God can deliver! Forgiveness in action causes us to move forward in the things of God. Philippians 3:13-14 says, *"Brothers, I count not myself to have apprehended: but this one thing I do, forgetting those things which are behind, and reaching forth to those things which are before, I press toward the mark for the prize of the high calling of God in Christ Jesus."*

The word "forgetting" in this text means to *"erase out of memory."* Thus, the word is not implying that you forget the incident as if it never happened. However, the pain that is associated with the incident is what is erased. When we apply this principle to our lives, we can forgive just as the Lord has forgiven us. It is imperative to note that we cannot forgive with our mind. Forgiveness, must come from the heart. It is the love of God that empowers us to forgive.

> *God forgave us for all of our sins and demonstrated His love towards us when He sent Yeshua to die in our place: "For God so loved the world that he gave his one and only Son,[a] that whoever believes in him shall not perish but have eternal life" (John 3:16).*

In today's society, over 75% of all marital, family, and health problems manifest from a root of unforgiveness. Because of unforgiveness, relationships have been terminated prematurely, and some believers have even died prematurely!

As I stated earlier in this chapter, unforgiveness opens doors for many other demons to come in and set-up residence in your life. Ask the Lord to show you who you need to forgive today. In addition to forgiving that person, you may also need to forgive yourself. In fact this may bring about the greatest release!

## 2. The Stronghold of *Anger*

It is imperative to note, that anger is a normal emotion. It is an emotion that even God possesses. History informs us that God became angry at Israel on many occasions. One occasion that comes to mind is found in Numbers 11:1-3:

> *And when the people complained, it displeased the LORD: and the LORD heard it; and his anger was kindled; and the fire of the LORD burnt among them, and consumed them that were in the uttermost parts of the camp. ²And the people cried unto Moses; and when Moses prayed unto the LORD, the fire was quenched. ³And he called the name of the place Taberah: because the fire of the LORD burnt among them.*

This passage of Scripture gives us a vivid picture of what happens when God becomes angry. He became so angry with the people that He released His consuming fire. Webster defines anger as *"a strong emotion; a feeling that is oriented toward some real or supposed grievance."*

To get a clear perception of this emotion, we need to identify it in two categories. Anger that is selfish and uncontrollable is described as *unjustifiable anger*. This type of anger can sometimes turn into rage, which opens up portals for demonic influences to manifest such as a "spirit of murder." We see a picture of this type of anger manifested through Cain in Genesis 4:4-8:

> *But Abel brought fat portions from some of the firstborn of his flock. The LORD looked with favor on Abel and his offering, 5 but on Cain and his offering he did not look with favor. So Cain was very angry, and his face was downcast. 6 Then the LORD said to Cain, "Why are you angry? Why is your face downcast? 7 If you do what is right, will you not be accepted? But if you do not do what is right, sin is crouching at your door; it desires to have you, but you must master it. 8 Now Cain said to his brother Abel, "Let's go out to the field." And while they were in the field, Cain attacked his brother Abel and killed him.*

Cain's anger became uncontrollable because of his jealousy towards his brother. So we see what can happen when you allow your anger to get out of control. Now the Bible does not indicate that anger is a sin. In Ephesians 4:26-27, Paul makes a clear distinction between anger and sin: *"Be ye angry, and sin not: let not the sun go down on your wrath: Neither give place to the devil."*

This text indicates to us that we will experience anger on this Christian journey. However, if your anger becomes uncontrollable it can lead to sin. When anger becomes uncontrollable, it can turn into rage, as we observed with Cain. Anger under control does not necessarily mean that the issue that provoked you to become angry has been resolved. Controlling your anger, however, closes the door to the enemy.

Let me show you how anger builds up. When you suppress your anger, it builds up like a pressure gauge. Under too much pressure, the gauge will eventually burst. The best remedy for controlling your anger is prayer and meditating on the Word of God. As intimacy becomes evident in your relationship with God, temperance will manifest in your behavior. We know that temperance (self control) is one of the fruit of the Spirit mentioned in Galatians 5:22. However, if you continue to suppress your anger it can be passed down to another generation.

I had an opportunity to counsel a young woman who had seven children by the age of 39. We will call her Angel (not her real name). Angel had a serious problem with anger. Angel was aware of this problem, but because she had not totally surrendered her life to God, her anger consumed her. When Angel was provoked to anger whatever was in her heart would come out of her mouth. Angel was not aware that her anger was tearing apart her relationship with her children and everyone else in her world.

During the counseling session the Lord revealed to Angel that she needed to forgive someone in her past. Angel confessed that she was a victim of emotional abuse from her father. As I continued to counsel Angel, I discovered that the spirit of anger was part of a generational curse that had been passed down from her father. I also had the opportunity to pray for Angel and her children. Of her seven children, the spirit of anger had victimized four. I told Angel that we had to break this generational curse of anger off of her family. This was an issue that Angel had to confront if she was going to walk in wholeness. Today, Angel has been set free and has eradicated the curse that was upon her seed.

Another category of anger is justifiable anger. This type of anger is defined as fair and reasonable given the circumstances. An example of this type of anger is depicted in Mark 11:15-18:

> *15And they come to Jerusalem: and Jesus went into the temple, and began to cast out them that sold and bought in the temple, and overthrew the tables of the moneychangers, and the seats of them that sold doves; 16And would not suffer that any man should carry any vessel through the temple. 17And he taught, saying unto them, Is it not written, My house shall be called of all nations the house of prayer? but ye have made it a den of thieves. 18And the scribes and chief priests heard it, and sought how they might destroy him: for they feared him, because all the people was astonished at his doctrine.*

When Jesus witnessed the merchants selling in the temple He became angry and overthrew their tables.

The merchants' purpose for utilizing the temple is what provoked Jesus to anger. His anger caused him to manifest a behavior that they had not seen. I am sure when Jesus overthrew the tables it was not done in meekness. Jesus anger was demonstrated and was necessary because the merchants had dishonored the temple. Why? They did not use the temple for the purpose it existed.

We know from Bible history that the temple was to be a place where the Jews would come to worship. Jesus said that it should be a *"House of Prayer"* to all nations. Yet, the merchants turned it into a shopping mall. Therefore, this type of anger was a righteous or justifiable anger. However, as believers we must be very meticulous about using justifiable anger for our own gain. Many churches are starting to utilize the "Anger Management" module in their churches, which is helping members to overcome their anger. As Christians we must not allow our anger to transcend the love of God. Love is the greatest gift!

### 3.   The Stronghold of *Pride*

If our perception of pride is going to be clear, we must observe it's origin in the Scriptures. Of all God's creation, Lucifer was the most spectacular. Ezekiel writes that he was clothed with every precious stone and he walked on the holy mountain of God. Lucifer was described as *"the model of perfection, full of wisdom and perfect in beauty"* (Ezekiel 28:12 NIV). God put Lucifer in a strategic position for His glory.

But Lucifer compromised his position, realized his own wisdom and beauty, and pride crept in. Ezekiel 28:17 records God's assessment of Lucifer's sin. He says, *"Your heart became proud on account of your beauty, and you corrupted your wisdom because of your splendor. So I threw you to the earth; I made a spectacle of you before kings.*

The Hebrew word for pride is "go-bah," which means *"arrogance, high, pride."* The Prophet Isaiah informs us that pride in the heart of Lucifer made him overestimate who he was. Pride destroyed him, as evidenced by his declaration that he would be like the Most High God (Isaiah 14:12-14):

> *How art thou fallen from heaven, O Lucifer, son of the morning! how art thou cut down to the ground, which didst weakened the nations! For Thou has said in thine heart, I will ascend into heaven, I will exalt my throne above the stars of God: I will sit also upon the mount of the congregations, in the sides of the north: I will ascend above the heights of the clouds; I will be with the most High.*

We know that the name Lucifer is another name that is used for Satan. This passage of Scripture clearly identifies how pride took root in his heart. As we can see, pride will ultimately lead to self-deception. Satan did not have a throne but yet indicates that he will exalt his throne above the stars of God.

Let's look at some passages in Proverbs dealing with the spirit of pride and what effects it produces:

- *Pride goes before destruction, a haughty spirit before a fall* (Proverbs 16:18).

- *When pride comes, then comes shame: but with the lowly is wisdom* (Proverbs 11:12).

- *Before destruction the heart of man is haughty, and before honor is humility* (Proverbs 18:12).

The Bible says that God resists the proud and give grace to the humble. When we subject ourselves to the spirit of pride, we become self-righteous and self-sufficient. This type of behavior implies that we are in control of our lives. God wants us to totally surrender every area of our life to Him. The spirit of pride is more evident to others than ourselves. In other words, you can never see the spirit operating in you because of your own self-righteousness. I heard one preacher say that, "Pride is like bad breath. You are the last one to know that you have it!"

No matter how anointed we think we are, we must daily put on the garment of humility. We must not forget that it is God who has made us who we are today. We must always remember to give God the Glory for all that He does through us. Don't let people cause you to be puffed up. I remember when God exposed the spirit of pride in me. God was using me mightily in the church. People would always come up to me and tell me that when I prayed, the heavens literally opened up. God had given me grace with my pastor and I was given the assignment to pray before the congregation every Sunday morning before the service began. Some pastors called this "Morning Glory." As I prayed the power of God was released and the atmosphere was conducive for the Holy Spirit to move in an unprecedented way.

In the midst of my receiving accolades from the people of God, I opened the door for a spirit of pride. I knew that when I prayed the heavens were going to open. I felt like I was the only vessel in the church that God could use to "open heaven." Yes, the spirit of pride was rooted in my heart. The Lord revealed this spirit to me and it was rooted in my heart. It was ugly. The Lord used a circumstance that occurred with my youngest daughter to humble me. I realized that God had not only extended grace to me with the pastor, but also his people.

I was a respected leader in the church. However, God used a circumstance that occurred with my youngest daughter to humble me. My youngest daughter whom I trained in the admonition of the Lord got pregnant out of wedlock. I had prayed and believed that I broke this generational curse off my seed. I lived a life of celibacy before my children and I was hoping and praying that the mantle would fall on them. As a result of this incident a spirit of shame was upon me that I could not shake. Although, the intercessory team discerned something was wrong with me, they failed to identify what spirit was holding me captive.

I remember one Sunday the pastor's armor bearer came to me, laid hands on me, and breaking that spirit off of me. The Lord let me know that she was able to identify the spirit because she had been delivered from the spirit of shame in her past. The yoke was destroyed because of the anointing. I learned to "humble" myself and to daily put on the garment of humility. I learned how to give God the Glory for all that He does through me. The Lord is clear when he states, *"I will not give my Glory to another"* (Isaiah 48:11).

### *The Altar of Confession*

The word "altar" is used in the Bible several times and has various meanings. The first occurrence of the word in the Old Testament is in Genesis 8:20, which reads: *"And Noah builded an altar unto the LORD; and took of every clean beast, and of every clean fowl, and offered burnt offerings on the altar."* The altar was an elevated structure used for the sacrifice of animals.

The greatest sacrifice that we can offer to God is our bodies. We have been instructed to present our bodies a living sacrifice (Romans 12:1). Therefore, the altar is a place where we are to crucify everything that is not like God. It is the place where we identify the issues in our hearts.

As God reveals them to us, we can no longer walk in denial as if they did not exist. It is imperative to note that both wickedness and conviction originate in the heart. The altar of confession always deals with conviction. As the Holy Spirit convicts us, we are instructed by God to confess our faults and sins: *"Confess your faults one to another, and pray one for another, that ye may be healed. The effectual fervent prayer of a righteous man availed much"* (James 5:16). We are told that if we confess our sins, *"...he is faithful and just to forgive us our sins, and to cleanse us from all unrighteousness"* (1 John 1:9).

Unfortunately, many believers struggle to confide with those in the Body of Christ because of a violation of trust they may have experienced in the past. Consequently, God has placed the five-fold ministry gifts in the church and part of their assignment is to counsel God's people, and give instruction according to His Word. We must trust God in them and be able to come to them and receive prayer in those areas where we have issues. Our pastors are watchmen over our souls, and God is holding every man and woman in a position of leadership accountable for any destruction of their "sheep."

Going back to the text, the word "fault" in the Greek is interpreted as a "shortcoming" or "weakness." The word does not imply that you have entered into sin, however, if the weakness is not rectified it could lead to sin. The Bible says it is the little foxes that spoil the vine (Song of Solomon 2:15). As we confess daily to God, we are acknowledging that we are ready to receive His deliverance. The first step to your deliverance is repentance. True repentance involves alienation (turning away) from the thing that caused you to sin. It literally means to change direction, and to change your mind. King David gives us an example of true repentance in Psalm 51:

*Have mercy upon me, O God, according to thy lovingkindness: according unto the multitude of thy tender mercies blot out my transgressions. Wash me throughly from mine iniquity, and cleanse me from my sin. For I acknowledge my transgressions: and my sin is ever before me.*

*Against thee, thee only, have I sinned, and done this evil in thy sight: that thou mightest be justified when thou speakest, and be clear when thou judgest. Behold, I was shapen in iniquity; and in sin did my mother conceive me. Behold, thou desirest truth in the inward parts: and in the hidden part thou shalt make me to know wisdom. Purge me with hyssop, and I shall be clean: wash me, and I shall be whiter than snow. Make me to hear joy and gladness; that the bones which thou hast broken may rejoice. Hide thy face from my sins, and blot out all mine iniquities.*

*Create in me a clean heart, O God; and renew a right spirit within me. Cast me not away from thy presence; and take not thy Holy Spirit from me. Restore unto me the joy of thy salvation; and uphold me with thy free spirit. Then will I teach transgressors thy ways; and sinners shall be converted unto thee. Deliver me from bloodguiltiness, O God, thou God of my salvation: and my tongue shall sing aloud of thy righteousness. O Lord, open thou my lips; and my mouth shall shew forth thy praise. For thou desirest not sacrifice; else would I give it: thou delightest not in burnt offering. The sacrifices of God are a broken spirit: a broken and a contrite heart, O God, thou wilt not despise. Do good in thy good pleasure unto Zion: build thou the walls of Jerusalem. Then shalt thou be pleased with the sacrifices of righteousness, with burnt offering and whole burnt offering: then shall they offer bullocks upon thine altar. - Psalms 51*

Yes, it is true that King David was a murderer and adulterer, however, he is not known for those acts, but rather as being a man after God's heart. King David was a man with many issues. However his love for God brought him to a place of humility that caused him to acknowledge every sin that separated him from God. He was thoroughly convinced that he could not live without God's presence.

David's cry in Psalms 51 depicts a heart filled with godly sorrow that wants to be cleansed and restored back to the place of fellowship with God. Because David acknowledged his sin, God healed and restored him. Beloved, the one key word in this passage that I want you to focus on is "acknowledged." When true repentance takes place, restoration and transformation will follow.

I stated earlier in the chapter that many believers are in bondage as a result of inner issues not being resolved. Whenever there is a reoccurring issue in your spirit, this is an indication that the issue is unresolved. In order for the issue to be resolved you must first acknowledge that it exists. The next step is to confront it! I do realize that some issues in our heart are more painful than others. But God will give you the grace to overcome. Remember it is in the inner man where the strongman sets up residence. If we do not bind the strongman from the root, we are merely going through the motion of deliverance and not truly experiencing it.

Ask yourself the following question: *"What is the root of my anger?"* It could be offense, bitterness, or even jealousy. Are you tired of attending church Sunday, after Sunday and yet there is no change? Unfortunately, this is the testimony of many believers. We will never be whom God has called us to be if we do not allow the pruning process to take place in our lives. Beloved, it is time to make a spiritual assessment. What ever has hindered you from moving forward in God, address the issue today!

## *Application: Restoration of the Inner Man*

After reading this chapter, you are now accountable to respond to the truth and insight that God has revealed to you. The Word declares that we will know the *truth* and the *truth* will make us free (John 4:24).

Today, God wants to release you from the issues that we have identified, which may include unforgiveness, anger, and pride. He also wants to deliver you from other personal strongholds that I may not have identified, but which the Holy Spirit will expose. You know what you are struggling with on the inside. You and the Holy Spirit know what they are! God is going to deliver you and release the wind of the Spirit upon you to bring great deliverance! Pray this prayer and allow the ministry of the Holy Spirit to take you to another dimension of Kingdom living!

> *Father, I come in the Name of Jesus, asking that you search my heart. I desire truth in the inner man, and I ask that you deliver me from every stronghold (name them). I receive your forgiveness and I forgive those who have trespassed against me. Thank you for restoring my mind and I declare that I have the mind of Christ today. Thank you for your unconditional love that is exemplified in my life. Thank you for your grace*

*that is sufficient to me today! Lord, as I walk towards my destiny and purpose I ask that you continue to wash me with the Blood of Jesus and cleanse me from all unrighteousness. I bind every tormenting spirit in the name of Jesus. I decree and declare that I am delivered from unforgiveness and healed from the hurts of my past. I decree and declare that I am pressing toward the mark of the high call in Christ Jesus. I walk in victory in every area of my life. In Jesus Name I pray. AMEN*

*~Worship is the highest form of prayer. It is the place where your intimacy with God causes Him to impregnate you with a seed of vision and purpose for your life, and at the appointed time YOU shall birth forth His promises~*

## Chapter 3

# WORSHIP: THE PLACE OF CONCEPTION

One of the most told stories in the Bible has to do with a woman in the New Testament who is not identified by name. In John 4:20-24 we find the account of Jesus conversing with this woman as they sat at Jacob's well. She was so significant to the Lord that He took a detour just to meet her. The passage reads:

*Our fathers worshiped on this mountain, but you Jews claim that the place where we must worship is in Jerusalem." Jesus declared, "Believe me, woman, a time is coming when you will worship the Father neither on this mountain nor in Jerusalem. You Samaritans*

*worship what you do not know; we worship
what we do know, for salvation is from the
Jews. Yet a time is coming and has now come
when the true worshipers will worship the
Father in spirit and truth, for they are the
kind of worshipers the Father seeks. God is
spirit, and his worshipers must worship in
spirit and in truth.*

She is identified as a Samaritan woman. This
dialogue between her and Jesus is very interesting.
They delve into a variety of topics. For the purpose
of this chapter, we will focus on their discussion of
worship.

We know that the Jews and the Samaritans were at
enmity one with the other. Their differences included
perspectives on worship. As they talk, Jesus brings
clarity to the definition of true worship. The woman
conveys to Jesus how her forefathers worshipped
on the mountain for many years. It is clear that the
Samaritans and Jews perception of worship had to do
with location. Jesus conveys to the woman that true
worship is not predicated on location.

It does not matter if you worship on the mountain
or in Jerusalem. Nor does it matter if you worship in
the temple or in your living room. True worship must
come from the heart. In this passage of Scripture Jesus
makes a clear distinction as to the type of worship the
Father desires. Why was this necessary? Could it be
that there are other types of worship that believers

73

are engaging in? The Bible identifies three types of worship that Jesus considers to be unacceptable:

1. **Vain Worship** – *"Howbeit in vain do they worship me, teaching for doctrines the commandments of men."* (Mark 7:7 KJV). When we follow the doctrines of men instead of the Word of God, our worship becomes vain and empty.

2. **Idol Worship** – *"Thou shalt not make unto thee any graven image, or any likeness of any thing that is in heaven above, or that is in the earth beneath, or that is in the water under the earth."* (Exodus 20:4 KJV). God commands us not to engage in this type of worship. Idol worship takes place when we worship images, people, or any other created thing. It can be anything that you put before God, including your spouse, children, career, or vehicles.

3. **Worship of Angels** – *"Let no man beguile you of your reward in a voluntary humility and worshipping of angels, intruding into those things which he hath not seen, vainly puffed up by his fleshly mind, And not holding the Head, from which all the body by joints and bands having nourishment ministered, and knit together, increaseth with the increase of God."* (Colossians 2:18-19 KJV). God has made us a little lower than angels, and we have been instructed not to worship them. We will find

this command in the book of Revelation, when John receives an overwhelming vision from the Lord. John began to worship the angel and was rebuked. Revelation 19:10 reads: *"At this I fell at his feet to worship him. But he said to me, 'Do not do it! I am a fellow servant with you and with your brothers who hold to the testimony of Jesus. Worship God! For the testimony of Jesus is the spirit of prophecy.'"*

God is very adamant about who we direct our worship to. He is our Creator. He created us to glorify Him. God alone is worthy of our worship! When we acknowledge this truth we will worship Him alone!

### *The Process of Conception*

The Bible reveals to us in the book of Genesis how God created man from the dust of the ground. The Scripture reads: *"And the LORD God formed man of the dust of the ground, and breathed into his nostrils the breath of life, and the man became a living being."* (Genesis 2:7, NIV). This is an awesome revelation of God's creativity. In God's creativity, He designs the woman, pulling her out of the rib of man. Therefore, we have the first manifestation of woman, whom we know as Eve.

Now, we will observe in Bible history how a shift takes place as Eve gives birth to the second man. This man is her son, who was named Cain. What was the shift that took place? After God pulled the woman out of the rib of man, in essence all of mankind came out of the womb of the woman. So the woman is now a producer. God, Author of Life, uses the woman to give birth to life. What an amazing gift that God has given to the woman - the ability to bring forth life! God is revealing to us that there is a significant correlation between true worship and conception.

We have often heard the statement referring to the "joy of childbearing." The joy, however, is not experienced in the actual giving of birth. I have not yet heard of a woman who is giving birth actually praising God as the labor pains manifest. The joy comes when the child is presented to her –joy unspeakable!

Now, let's look at the word "conception" and get clarity concerning its meaning. Conception is defined as the uniting of the egg and sperm. Before the egg and sperm connect, the process of ovulation must take place. Most pregnancies are not planned. Therefore, it is imperative to understand this process if you are planning a pregnancy. Ovulation is the release of a single, mature egg from the ovarian follicle. The human ovary produces a multitude of ova during the course of a month, the largest of which is expelled into the pelvic cavity and swept into the Fallopian tube. When the woman ovulates she is fertile and is now in a position for conception to take place.

To be fertile means to be in a position to produce. Why would God give us this analogy of conception with the woman in the natural? So that He can give us insight to what takes places in the realm of the spirit when one conceives. God is revealing to us today how natural conception is similar to spiritual conception. God said that many of His children are having foreplay with Him. Now, we know that in order to become pregnant in the natural, we must go beyond foreplay. There must be an intimate connection with our spouse if we are going to conceive.

It is the same in the spirit. Before God can impregnate us with His seed we must become intimate with Him. God uses the relationship between a man and woman to describe the type of relationship that He is seeking from His children. The Scripture says in Genesis 4:1, *"And Adam knew Eve his wife; and she conceived, and bore Cain, and said, I have gotten a man from the LORD."*

In this verse, the English word "knew" is the Hebrew word "yada," which means *"to know, or recognize, or be acquainted with."* The word suggests a very close intimacy, as a husband and wife are intimate in marriage. It indicates experiential, not just, theoretical knowledge. In other words, you cannot know God without a personal experience. As we see in the above verse, after Adam and Eve became intimate, she conceived. Before conception can manifest, intimacy must be evident. Unfortunately, many Christians have become too passive concerning their relationship with God.

God is not looking for part-time lovers. He desires intimacy from us. If you want intimacy with Him, you must pursue it. This word is for you, the reader. If you draw nigh to God, He will draw nigh to you. In other words, God will reveal Himself to you. You must understand that intimacy comes with a price. Are you willing to pay the price to enhance your relationship with God? It is clear from Deuteronomy 6:5 that God desires intimacy: *"And thou shalt love the LORD thy God with all thine heart, and with all thy soul, and with all thy might."*

This passage of Scripture instructs us to love God with all of our being. When we truly love God, it will be demonstrated in our every day lives. God said that if we love Him we would obey Him (John 14:15). Obedience to His Word will thrust you into intimacy. When we become intimate with God we put ourselves in a position to become pregnant with His seed and at His appointed time, we can birth His purpose and plans for our lives.

Beloved, God has a plan for you. He reveals this truth to us in Jeremiah 29:11: *"For I know the thoughts and plans that I have for you, says the Lord, thoughts and plans for welfare and peace and not for evil, to give you hope in your final outcome." (AMP).* When the seed is placed in our womb (the spirit man), it has to be nurtured. In order for the seed to germinate we must nurture the seed with the necessary ingredients that will bring increase. These ingredients will include prayer, fasting, and releasing your faith in the Word of God. When we appropriate the necessary ingredients we will have a clear vision of God's purpose and plans for our lives. We will move forward towards our destiny so that we can maximize our full potential.

I am reminded of my childhood participation in a neighborhood Salvation Army. The pastor would come and pick up children whose parents wanted them to go to church. Although, my mother would insist that I go to the good old traditional Baptist church with her, she knew that there was something about that neighborhood church that drew my attention. Therefore, she faithfully made sure I was ready to be picked up every Sunday. The pastor and Sunday school teachers were diligent in teaching me about Christ and along with my mother, helped to lay a good foundation for my life.

I accepted the Lord at an early age. Like most of us, I went out into the world to experience it. I got myself in an ungodly relationship that only the power of God could deliver me out of. I made a vow to the Lord that if He would deliver me out of this relationship I would totally surrender my life to Him. Well, God answered my prayer and set me free from a lifestyle of bondage. He revealed to me what I must do if I was to fulfill my purpose and destiny. He told me that He created me for relationship, and He had to be first in my life. He told me that he was a jealous God and was not interested in being a part-time lover. He demanded intimacy from me.

How was I to accomplish this intimacy that God was requiring? First, I had to make a commitment that I would live for God. Paul puts it like this in the Scriptures: *"I am crucified with Christ: nevertheless I live; yet not I, but Christ liveth in me: and the life which I now live in the flesh I live by the faith of the Son of God, who loved me, and gave himself for me."* (Galatians 2:20).

I had to come to the conclusion that I no longer lived for me, but for Christ. When I surrendered my life to Him, I began to take on His characteristics and attributes. Since we have been created in His image, there should be something about us that resembles the Lord. If we have His DNA shouldn't we look like Him? Think about it. If your biological children did not look like you wouldn't you think something was wrong?

### *Characteristics of True Worship*

In John 4:24 we find the word "worship." It is taken from the Greek word *"proskuneo,"* which means *"to bow down."* Bowing down or bending the knee is an act of submission to a higher deity, and is a demonstration of true humility. The Bible instructs us to humble ourselves under the hand of Almighty God (I Peter 5:6). In Biblical history, when cultures wanted to show respect and honor to those in authority, it was customary for them to bow down. We see examples of this homage as people bowed before kings.

In the Old Testament, as the priest entered into the "Holy of Holies," they would bow down before "*Adonai.*" Some would even lay prostrate in the presence of the Lord. It was clear that they reverenced the Lord as they demonstrated total submission to Him. This type of reverence for God is not present in most of our churches today.

A few years ago, I conducted a survey on worship in our churches. I found out that our concept of worship needed to be redefined. I ascertained that many believers that come to church participated in the worship program, but never experienced the essence of true worship. Why? My survey concluded that over half of those that came to church on Sunday did not have a relationship with God. If you do not know God, how can you truly worship Him? Many believers religiously go to church Sunday after Sunday as a formality and out of tradition. Beloved, religion can never fill the void or emptiness that mankind experiences. Every human being was created with a void that only God can fill.

True worship opens the heavens, and emanates from a heart that loves God. Do you know what would happen if believers came together and worshipped the Lord in Spirit and in truth? God would move in an unprecedented way! The gifts of the Spirit would be stirred up and angels would be in our midst. The Glory Cloud would hover over us as we worship the Most High God. When the heavens are opened, we experience on earth what is taking place in heaven.

The Word of God lets us know that God sits high on the throne.

In Revelation 7:11 we see a picture of what is taking place around the throne of God. The Word says, *"And all the angels stood round about the throne, and about the elders and the four beasts, and fell before the throne on their faces, and worshipped God."* When authentic worship takes place, we literally connect to what is already taking place in heaven. As we connect, we bring the glory from heaven to earth. When the glory of God is released we experience the manifest presence of God. We are literally transformed into His image and we began to look like Him.

Many of the prophets of today have confirmed that God is restoring the Tabernacle of David. This is a prophetic word that was first spoken in Amos 9:11 and later in the New Testament: *"After this I will return, and will build again the tabernacle of David, which is fallen down; and I will build again the ruins thereof, and I will set it up:"* (Acts 15:16).

We can see a manifestation of this prophecy today, as God uses His people to worship in various ways. I had the opportunity to attend a praise and worship conference where I witnessed prophetic dancers ministering the heart of God. God used them to express His heart in artistic and prophetic worship. As they ministered unto the Lord, the Glory of God manifested and angelic beings were present. True worship exuded out of the hearts of God's people that produced an atmosphere that caused the heavens to explode! This is the Davidic worship that God is manifesting in this hour.

### *True Worship emanates from our Spirit, not the Flesh*

One Sunday while visiting a church in the Dallas/ Fort Worth metroplex area, I witnessed a statement presented in error by the worship leader. As he began to exhort the Body of Christ to enter into the presence of God, he stated how it was a privilege afforded to everyone. He stated that he had found no place in the Bible indicating that sinners could not worship God. Well, of course I did not go up to the man after the service and attempt to correct him. That would have been out of order. After all I was just a visitor. However, I prayed and asked God to teach him how to rightly divide the Word of Truth because I believe that statement was presented in ignorance. God said in His Word *"My people are destroyed for lack of knowledge..."* (Hosea 4:6).

The Word of God states that God is a spirit and they that worship Him must worship Him in Spirit and in truth. If I were to challenge the statement made by the worship leader, my first argument would be that sinners couldn't worship God because they are spiritually dead. Only when we become Born Again can we worship God. In John 14:6, Jesus said, *"...I am the way, the truth, and the life: no man cometh unto the Father, but by me."* If we are going to worship in truth, our focus must be centered on Christ.

Jesus has reconciled us back to the Father. This was accomplished through His death, burial, and resurrection. Now we can have fellowship with God. This was God's original plan for mankind. We were created to have fellowship with Him. When we become Born Again, a process takes place called *regeneration*. Our spiritual man, which was at one time dead because we were sinners separated from God, now becomes alive. We are now able to commune with God. As we yield to the Holy Spirit, He enables and empowers us to worship God. Therefore, worship is not predicated on emotionalism. Although, our emotions are evident in worship, they are not evidence that we are having a true worship experience.

The Word declares that the flesh is enmity towards God, and they that walk in the flesh cannot please Him, even though, some believers go to church every Sunday and attempt to do so. Unfortunately, they leave their place of worship empty, because they were unsuccessful in their attempt to connect with God in the flesh. When we worship God in spirit and in truth we get into the presence of God. As I stated in the first chapter of this book, everybody can praise God. The Bible says, *"Let everything that has breath praise the Lord..."* (Psalms 150:6). However, only those who have been Born Again can experience worship. If we are going to enter into the Holies of Holies we must exit the courts of praise and the gates of thanksgiving. For many believers this is their dwelling place. Fresh oil and new wine flow from the throne room when we get into His presence.

Everything that we need is in the presence of God. If you need healing, get in His presence. I remember one occasion when I was at church I had to endure the excruciating pain of a toothache. I was determined not to allow the pain distract me from ministering unto the Lord. I began to lift my hands to the Lord and worship Him. We stayed in worship for some time. I noticed that when worship concluded, my pain had subsided. The pain could not persist in the presence of God. Why? When you get into the presence of God, everything that is not like Him will be consumed. Remember, we stated earlier that when true worship manifests we bring the glory from heaven to earth! There is no pain in heaven. Therefore, I was healed of the toothache with the excruciating pain. To God be the Glory!

### *True Worship Manifests from a Lifestyle of Holiness*

In the Old Testament God used the tabernacle as a place for Israel to come and worship Him. The high priest represented the Jews before God. There was an order established before they could enter. The Jews understood the authority of the high priest and how they had to submit to that authority before entering the tabernacle. Remember - the Old Testament is a shadow of what God has given us today through

Christ. Today, the Lord Jesus is the High Priest of a more perfect tabernacle. Hebrews 9:11-12 reveals this truth:

*But Christ being come an high priest of good things to come, by a greater and more perfect tabernacle, not made with hands, that is to say, not of this building; Neither by the blood of goats and calves, but by his own blood he entered in once into the holy place, having obtained eternal redemption for us.*

Because of what Christ has done for us, when we become a Christian we become the temple of God, where His spirit can dwell. In order for the Holy Spirit to dwell in us, our temple must be clean. We have been given explicit instructions not to defile the temple. Paul addresses the Corinthian church along these lines as he gives this directive in 1 Corinthians 3:16-17: *"Know ye not that ye are the temple of God, and that the Spirit of God dwelleth in you? If any man defile the temple of God, him shall God destroy; for the temple of God is holy, which temple ye are."*

Paul was asking them a question. In layman's terms, this is what Paul was asking them: *"Do you not know that you are the temple in which the Spirit of God dwells?"* I present that same question to you today. If you are a Christian you have been bought with a price. The Word says in Galatians 3:13 that Christ has redeemed us from the curse of the law. The Word "redeemed" means to *"purchase or buy back."* Now, when you purchase something, you become the owner. Therefore, as Christians we now belong to Christ. Since we belong to Him we should be dancing to His tune. Let me enlighten you on what it means to defile the temple.

First, you need to perceive that a temple is defined as a building or structure consecrated to the worship of a deity. We received revelation in 1 Corinthians 3:16-17 that we are the temple of God and He is the deity that we are to worship. The word "defile" in the Greek means to *"corrupt, ruin, or deprave."* Listen to what Jesus says that defiles the temple in Mark 7:20-23:

> *And He said, "What comes out of a man, that defiles a man.* [21] *For from within, out of the heart of men, proceed evil thoughts, adulteries, fornications, murders,* [22] *thefts, covetousness, wickedness, deceit, lewdness, an evil eye, blasphemy, pride, foolishness.* [23] *All these evil things come from within and defile a man.*

Jesus brings clarity to what really defiles the temple. It is not what we consume, but what's in our hearts. We talked about the issues in our heart in Chapter two and how imperative it is for us to allow the Holy Spirit to expose them so that we can live a holy life before the Lord. If we are going to worship the Lord in the beauty of holiness we must have a clear perception of this attribute. Holiness means to be set apart, or separated for God's use. Unfortunately, in many of our churches today there is a lack of holiness. There are those who profess to be Christians, but yet live contrary to the Word of God.

In this hour, God is thrusting forth apostolic ministries who are raising up the standard of holiness. If we are going to reach this generation we must establish this standard back into the church. The Bible is clear that without holiness we cannot see God. Holiness is not something we try to implement at a Sunday morning service. Holiness is a lifestyle. We cannot live like heathens through the week, and come to church on Sunday and expect to worship the Lord in the beauty of holiness. The Bible instructs us not to grieve the Holy Spirit. He is grieved when we do not live holy lives. Ask yourself this question. What is the Holy Spirit doing while I am engaging in the following activities?

- Lying
- Smoking and drinking
- Having sex outside of marriage
- Stealing on the job or from the IRS
- Committing Adultery
- Watching Pornography
- Engaging in homosexual activities
- Planting seeds of discord against your brethren
- Going to the club on Saturday, and at church on Sunday
- Rebelling against authority

- Disobeying the Word of God
- Inconsistency in paying tithes and giving offerings

If you are participating in any of these activities, the Holy Spirit is grieved. If we can grieve Him, this indicates to us that He has emotions. I don't know about you, but I do not want to grieve Him. What steps must we take to insure that we will not grieve the Holy Spirit? We must totally surrender to Him. Can we really live a life of holiness? Yes we can, because God would not ask us to do anything that He has not given us the ability to do. However we must adhere to the instructions in Romans 12:1-2:

*I beseech you therefore, brethren, by the mercies of God, that ye present your bodies a living sacrifice, holy, acceptable unto God, which is your reasonable service. And be not conformed to this world: but be ye transformed by the renewing of your mind, that ye may prove what is that good, and acceptable, and perfect, will of God.*

God is saying in this passage that we have to present our spirit, soul, and body to Him - our total being! This is a spiritual act of worship that we must implement on a daily basis. In the Old Testament, when the priest brought a sacrifice to God, the animal was dead. As we present our bodies to God as a living sacrifice we die to our flesh. As we die to our flesh, God will show us how to honor him with our bodies. It is imperative to note that we must study the Word of God consistently, if our mind is going to be renewed. When we become consistent in studying the Word and applying it to our lives then we began to look like Jesus. This is what we call *"transformation,"* which means, *"to be changed"!*

### True Worship Is Exemplified Through Our Giving

God does not need our money. The Bible lets us know that He owns everything. Psalms 24: 1 says, *"The earth is the LORD's, and the fullness thereof; the world, and they that dwell therein."* But as Christians, we need to understand that giving is a continuation of worship. When we are asked to bring our offering for some reason we tend to take our focus off of God and the giving becomes mechanical. We must perceive that when we bring an offering to the Lord, it is not something that we should do passively. We must worship the Lord with our money since He is the source of it.

When we worship the Lord with our money we demonstrate good stewardship. We acknowledge that we have because God has given. We acknowledge that He is *Jehovah-Jireh*, the God that provides. Therefore, when we are asked to pay our tithes, (the tenth of our income that we owe Him) and give an offering (something that you give above your tithes) we should give it cheerfully! The Bible declares that God loves a cheerful giver (2 Corinthians 9:7)! Believers should be excited about giving!

Giving is just another opportunity afforded to us for God to bless us abundantly. He said that if we give bountifully we would reap bountifully. Yet so many Christians continue to walk in defeat in this area. God demonstrated His love to us by giving. He gave His very best. One of the first Scriptures that we are taught as a child is John 3:16, which reads: *"For God so loved the world, that he gave his only begotten son, that whosoever believeth in him should not perish, but have everlasting life."*

It is clear from this Scripture that love will cause you to give. Because we love Him, we totally give our lives to Him. We apply this same principle with our assets. Although many believers confess that God has given them the power to get wealth, many will never experience it. Why? Because they have not surrendered their assets to the Lord! Luke 12:34 says "For where your treasure is, there will your heart be also. Our priority with our assets should be to advance the Kingdom of God. I have experienced the blessings of the Lord that makes one rich and adds no sorrow, as a result of my surrendering all my assets to the Lord.

God knows whom he can trust with his wealth. We have heard and received many prophecies of the wealth transfer. However, we must be in position to receive this transfer. Are you in position? Are you struggling to give to the God whom you say you love?

Is He Lord over your assets? These are all serious questions that we must ponder. Many believers are in bondage to "poverty" because they will not appropriate the tithing, giving, and sowing principle.

I was blessed to go to Dr. Cindy Trimm's conference in Florida in 2005. It was at this conference that God spoke a word to me and said that I would never be broke another day in my life. I remember Dr. Trimm asking those who desired to sow a $1000.00 offering to come up. I went to the altar and Dr. Trimm released a prophetic declaration over me that broke the spirit of poverty off my life. The next year I was sowing seeds of $1000.00 or more into the Kingdom of God. I had in my savings the money that I saved for a down payment on my house. The Lord spoke to me and told me to sow all of the money that I had saved for my house into the Kingdom. My love for God caused me to obey Him because I knew that if He wanted me to sow all of my savings, He had another plan.

At the beginning of the year I received many prophecies declaring that God was going to release me from my job and thrust me into full time ministry. It was evident from my traveling schedule that it was getting to be a burden to work a full time job and minister full time.

These prophetic words became a reality when God manifested a "suddenly" in my life. In August 2008, as I was closing on my home, I got laid-off from my job. It was a blessing! God answered my prayer. The

Lord certainly has a sense of humor! He blesses me with a home that He had built for me and then releases me from my job! God is Awesome! Oh yea, let me not forget to tell you that I purchased the home with no money down! In fact, I left the table with a check.

This is what sowing into God's Kingdom has done for me. When the Kingdom becomes "priority," things will follow your pursuit of His will for your life. The Scripture says in Matthew 6:33 *"But seek you first the kingdom of God, and his righteousness; and all these things shall be added to you."*

Beloved, you must get to a point in your life where giving is part of your worship! When you get to this place, God knows He can trust you so He will release more to you. I have learned to trust my God in all things. Truly the Lord enjoys taking care of His children. It has been nothing but a blessing, to be able to do the work of the ministry. I remember when I truly got revelation of the Kingdom and its benefits when I purchased Myles Monroe book *"Rediscovering the Kingdom."* It was like experiencing new birth all over again! God shared so much insight through him! This book is a must have for this generation. I got a new perspective on the message of the Kingdom. This is what I teach. I cannot get a way from it. Why? This is the central message of the Bible.

If we say we are Kingdom people we should live like it. God mandated us to take dominion over the earth. As Kingdom people we should have ownership. I have to share a little of this testimony. The same year that I got laid-off my job, I went to Canada. I heard Dr. Pat Francis at the beginning of 2008 and the Word that God spoke through her shifted me to Canada. I received an impartation there as well. God gave me a vision for several entities to create wealth.

- ***Longevity, Inc.*** – A Senior Citizens Activity Center

- ***Rainbow Productions*** - Gospel Plays and Christian Films

- ***CMS Enterprises*** – Consulting and Coaching

Yes, I received an impartation from great men and women of God that made my baby jump, and turn flips! Zion has travailed and vision and dreams have come forth! Now the irony of these testimonies is to get you the reader to understand that you must tithe, give, and sow into the Kingdom. Even in the midst of famine we must continue to sow. We must not allow the world's circumstance to deter us from receiving God's promises by robbing Him in our tithes. We must not give sparingly, but continue to sow bountifully so that we can reap a bountiful harvest.

In the interim, we must remember that applying these principles in obedience to God's Word is what releases the blessings!

*~ God is raising up an army of intercessors
who know how to pray strategically
and maneuver in many dimensions of
intercession. There is a revival that will
usher in the rapture of the Church and it
will be birthed out by the emerging Kingdom
Intercessors.~*

## Chapter 4

# HOW TO SHIFT FROM PRAYER TO INTERCESSION

Throughout Bible history, we see that whenever God desired to transform a nation, He looked for an intercessor. In the Old Testament we find two Scripture references where God was looking for an intercessor.

The first reference is in the book of Ezekiel:

*And I sought for a man among them, that should make up the hedge, and stand in the gap before me for the land, that I should not destroy it: but I found none. Therefore have I poured out mine indignation upon them; I have consumed them with the fire of my wrath: their own way have I recompensed upon their heads, saith the Lord GOD* (Ezekiel 22:30-31).

It is clear from this passage of Scripture that God is seeking intercessors. *"Standing in the gap"* is a metaphor for committed intercession, referring to the gap between God and man that an intercessor tries to repair. Where were the intercessors at that time? Could it be that they were all at the temple conducting business as usual? Or maybe they were asleep like the disciples who were on the ship with Jesus. We know that the Jews, who are God's chosen people, had a history of perpetual disobedience and rebellion against God. While God never intends to destroy His people, sin must be judged. Because there were no intercessors available, God's judgment was released upon the land. In this instance God's wrath came upon the people.

The second reference is in Isaiah 59:16: *"And he saw that there was no man, and wondered that there was no intercessor: therefore his arm brought salvation unto him; and his righteousness, it sustained him."* It appears in this instance that God became the intercessor and averted his judgment. God's mercy prevailed over his fierce anger. I want you to understand how powerful intercessory prayer is, and how much it is needed. Beloved, God is looking for individuals who will make themselves available to stand in the gap for this generation. Are you willing to make the sacrifice to become an intercessor for the Lord? It has always been God's desire for mankind to be a part of his plans and purposes.

Webster defines the word "intercessor," as "*one who intercedes.*" To intercede means "*to go or pass between; to plead or make a request on behalf of another.*" The Hebrew word for "intercessor" is *paga', paw-gah'* which is translated as "*to fall (upon)*; *to encounter, meet, reach, make intercession.*" An intercessor is a Born Again believer who has accepted the call of God to intercede on behalf of someone else. Intercessors become a mediator for those for whom they pray. A mediator is a negotiator who acts as a link between parties.

I worked in the legal field for many years in various types of law. I can remember working as a legal secretary in family law several years ago. When a divorce petition was filed, couples were encouraged by the attorney to attend a meeting called "mediation." Its purpose was to introduce a third-party, the mediator, whose responsibility was to settle the conflict between the parties by negotiating a resolution that both parties agreed upon.

Jesus is our mediator and has settled the conflict that existed between mankind and God as a result of the fall. Through his death, burial, resurrection, and ascension, He has reconciled mankind back to God.

According to Hebrews 11:24, Jesus is the mediator of a new covenant, and his blood continues to speak for us today.

I remember when I accepted the call to pray. I really did not know how to pray, however there was a concept, which I will explain, that was implemented in our church that taught me the basic foundation of prayer.

### *The ACTS Concept*

Many Christians are very familiar with the acronym **ACTS**, (Adoration, Confession, Thanksgiving, and Supplication). It is has been a pattern that many believers have utilized in developing a lifestyle of prayer. The acronym introduces us to the different types of prayer we engage in. However, there is a difference between prayer and intercession. Although the terms "prayer" and "intercession" are often used interchangeably, they have different meanings. It is evident that all intercession is prayer, but not all prayer is intercession, as demonstrated by the ACTS concept.

- Prayer is communication with God - *There should be a two-way dialogue.*

- Intercession involves praying for someone else, and praying with a focus on a particular issue. You petition God on behalf of someone else. In other words, your focus is not on your own needs.

- Your plea is compassionate to the point that you identify with what you are praying for.

The following pattern of ACTS has been a part of the prayer life of many believers:

1. *Adoration* – We adore and acknowledge the majesty of God

2. *Confession* – We acknowledge our sins before him and ask forgiveness

3. *Thanksgiving* – We express our gratefulness to God for all that He has done

4. *Supplication* – We plead our earnest request to God to meet our needs

These are the different types of prayer that we utilize to empower our prayer life. However, if we are going to move into the next dimension of prayer, we must shift to intercession. We will find in the Word how intercession was demonstrated through God, Jesus, and the Holy Spirit. As we saw earlier in Isaiah 59:16, God became the intercessor because no one in the earth was available to accomplish this task. In the New Testament, we see Jesus as the Chief Intercessor in Hebrew 7:25: "*Wherefore he is able also to save them to the uttermost that come unto*

*God by him, seeing he ever liveth to make interces-sion for them.* " What a blessing to know that Jesus is at the right hand of the Father interceding for you and me at this very moment! Even while He was on His way to the Cross, Jesus made intercession for His disciples and those that would follow Him through the message that was preached by His disciples and followers.

I encourage you to read the entire chapter of John 17, which I refer to as the "The Lord's Prayer." It exemplifies a very powerful prayer of intercession. We will also find in the Scripture the Holy Spirit depicted as an intercessor. He literally prays for us because the Word states that in our weakness we really don't know what to pray for. However, Romans 8:26 says: *"Likewise the Spirit also helpeth our infir-mities: for we know not what we should pray for as we ought: but the Spirit itself maketh intercession for us with groanings which cannot be uttered."* When we are at a loss for words and do not know what to say, the Holy Spirit prays for us according to the will of God.

You can be assured that when the Holy Spirit prays through you, your prayers are being received. And if they are being received, they are being answered. We must rely totally on the Holy Spirit because we can do nothing in our own wisdom. One of our famous presidents, Abraham Lincoln, attested to this truth: *"I have been driven many times to my knees by the overwhelming conviction that I had nowhere else to go. My own wisdom, and that of all about me seemed insufficient for the day."*

## How Do We Shift?

I remember back in high school when my best friend got her first car. It was a 5-speed blue Volkswagon. She allowed her boyfriend to teach her how to drive this car. As I watched them on the parking lot, I could see the car jerking and wondered what was going on. The car kept stopping and moving and continued like this for about 20 minutes. Then all of a sudden she began driving the car as if she had been driving for a lifetime! I found out that her boyfriend gave her some basic instructions. She then implemented them, and was able to maneuver the 5-speed vehicle. As I was observing, my first thought was, *'this is challenging, learning how to drive a stick shift!'* Of course, I don't think I would have gotten a 5-speed stick to learn how to drive with! I would have preferred a car with automatic transmission.

The challenge with a 5-speed was that you had to become familiar with the clutch, and know how and when to change gears. This process was called shifting. If you did not know how to shift the gears, you would either depress the clutch too soon or too late, or release it too soon or too late. You might also accidentally strip the gears by shifting into the wrong one. Any or all of these violations might cause the car to jerk, or keep it from moving. In order for the vehicle to move properly, you must shift to the proper gear.

This is the same principle we must apply in prayer as we shift to intercession. To shift means *"to change in place and position."* Your prayer focus is no longer on your needs, but the needs of others. Remember, intercessory prayer is not about you! When you shift from prayer to intercession you began to stand in the gap for people, cities, and nations.

Many years ago, when I accepted the call to intercede, God gave me this mandate from 1 Timothy 2:1-4:

> *I exhort therefore, that, first of all, supplications, prayers, intercessions, and giving of thanks, be made for all men; For kings, and for all that are in authority; that we may lead a quiet and peaceable life in all godliness and honesty. For this is good and acceptable in the sight of God our Saviour; Who will have all men to be saved, and to come unto the knowledge of the truth.*

God spoke to me and said that praying for others would be my priority. I remember having a dream of a woman who was disfigured. Her body parts were scattered all around her. However, the head of the woman was not disfigured. The dream terrified me, and I began to inquire of the Lord for the interpretation. The Lord told me that the woman represented the body of Christ.

The body parts that I saw scattered represented those on the frontline who had been wounded in battle and fallen from grace, as a result of having no strategic prayer covering. The assignment of the enemy prevailed against them because there was no prayer shield to protect them. I understood why the head of this woman was not disfigured. The Word declares in Colossians 1:18 that Jesus is the Head of the Body, the Church.

After receiving interpretation of the dream the Lord mandated me to pray for those on the frontline and all those in authority. God later showed me an open vision of multitudes of people forming a circle around the earth. In the vision I saw people of every culture coming together to pray. The Lord said that this is the great army of Kingdom intercessors that have been preserved for this age. As they offered strategic prayer unto the Lord, I saw smoke ascend into the heavens. It was the smoke from the incense, which came with the prayers of the saints, which ascended up before God out of the angel's hand. (Revelation 8:4)

As we observed in 1 Timothy 2:1-4, Paul admonishes us to pray for our leaders. Why? Leaders have the power to influence people. For better or worse, people follow them. We should pray for our president, governors, senators, five-fold ministry gifts, and all those who are in authority. Instead of criticizing our leaders, let's pray for them! It is not feasible to lead a quiet and peaceable life in all godliness and honesty without this prayer shield. The ultimate purpose is for all of mankind to be saved and to come unto the knowledge of the truth. I want to draw your attention to an example of intercessory prayer, found in Genesis 18:20-27. We will find Abraham interceding for the two cities Sodom and Gomorrah. The Scripture reads:

*And the Lord said, because the cry of Sodom and Gomorrah is great, and because their sin is very grievous;*

*I will go down now, and see whether they have done altogether according to the cry of it, which is come unto me; and if not, I will know.*

*And the men turned their faces from thence, and went toward Sodom: but Abraham stood yet before the Lord.*

*And Abraham drew near, and said, Wilt thou also destroy the righteous with the wicked?*

*Peradventure there be fifty righteous within the city: wilt thou also destroy and not spare the place for the fifty righteous that are therein?*

*That be far from thee to do after this manner, to slay the righteous with the wicked: and that the righteous should be as the wicked, that be far from thee: Shall not the Judge of all the earth do right?*

*And the Lord said, If I find in Sodom fifty righteous within the city, then I will spare all the place for their sakes.*

*And Abraham answered and said, Behold now, I have taken upon me to speak unto the Lord, which am but dust and ashes.*

Here we see Abraham humbling himself before the Lord as he makes intercession for these two cities. Many of us are very familiar with what happened to Sodom and Gomorrah. I challenge you to read the entire chapter of Genesis 18 to get the fullness of the story. Abraham went back and forth with God, petitioning him not to destroy the cities. His final request was that if God find at least ten righteous people in the cities, that His mercy would prevail! Unfortunately, there were not even ten righteous people in the two cities! Therefore, the wrath of God was released upon Sodom and Gomorrah. Why? God had to judge the sin of these two cities. Nevertheless, I have often pondered how God would have responded had there been ten righteous people found in the cities.

Kingdom intercessors are willing to make the necessary sacrifice to avert God's judgment. In the interim, just as God dealt with the sin in Sodom and Gomorrah, He shall judge the sin that exists in America. However, it is the responsibility of Kingdom intercessors to plead with God for his mercy. Like Abraham interceded for Sodom and Gomorrah, we must continue to intercede for America that she will return back to her first love. For the Lord is saying to America, *"Therefore say thou unto them, Thus saith the LORD of hosts; Turn ye unto me, saith the LORD of hosts, and I will turn unto you, saith the LORD of hosts."* (Zechariah 1:3).

### *Kingdom Intercessors Arising!*

"God is thrusting forth a new breed of inter-cessors." They are called Kingdom intercessors. Kingdom intercessors are Born Again, Spirit-filled believers who've accepted God's call to intercede. Kingdom intercessors are disciplined in prayer, studying the Word of God, and fasting. They live consecrated lives, making themselves available to be a vessel through which God can birth His purposes and plans in the earth realm. Because they have grad-uated from the School of the Spirit, they know how to maneuver in different dimensions of intercession. They are militant, radical, and know how to engage in spiritual warfare. Here are a few characteristic traits of Kingdom intercessors:

1. They are skilled and trained intercessors that know how to receive a burden from the Lord and pray it through.

2. They have a clear perception of the "gospel of the Kingdom" which is the central message of the Bible. In other words, they have a "Kingdom" mentality.

3. They understand their kingly and priestly roles.

4. They are men and women of integrity and are accountable to leadership.

5. They are prosperous in every area of their lives and good stewards over all that God has entrusted to them.

Kingdom intercessors are uniting and networking around the globe, bringing their strategies together to effectively advance the Kingdom of God. I had the opportunity to host a corporate prayer gathering on National Day of Prayer, May 7, 2009, at Prayer Mountain in Dallas, Texas.

As we gathered at 5:00 a.m., it was a blessing to see so many in attendance that would make the early morning sacrifice. The Psalmist said, *"O God, thou art my God; early will I seek thee..."* (Psalm 63:1, KJV). The gathering was very fruitful as people from various cultures came together from throughout the DFW/Metroplex area. We did not deviate from the assignment that was given to us through the National Day of Prayer leader, Shirley Dobson. We came together in corporate repentance, worship, and intercession. God moved in an unprecedented way because the atmosphere was conducive for the "Kingdom agenda." Many of us were already in preparation for this day as we implemented a corporate fast. God had given us specific instructions and we stuck to His directives.

Kingdom intercessors understand the importance of yielding to the Holy Spirit so God's purposes and plans can manifest. They know how to maneuver in the Spirit and will not tolerate the manifestation of the flesh. The assignment was fulfilled as we prayed the promises and God's glory was revealed. We concluded with this prophetic word in Revelation 11:15: *"And the seventh angel sounded; and there were great voices in heaven, saying, The kingdoms of this world are become the kingdoms of our Lord, and of his Christ; and he shall reign for ever and ever."*

### The Assignment of Kingdom Intercessors

Both Old and New Testaments give us examples of how God used the prayers of ordinary men and women to birth His will in the earth. One example that I would like to focus our attention on is found in Acts 12:1-16. In this passage, we find the church coming together to pray for one of the disciples, whom we know as Peter. As you read this passage of Scripture you will understand the assignment that was given to the church and how their fervency in prayer suddenly manifested a breakthrough:

Now about that time Herod the king
stretched forth his hands to vex certain of the
church.

²*And he killed James the brother of John
with the sword.*

³*And because he saw it pleased the Jews,
he proceeded further to take Peter also. (Then
were the days of unleavened bread.)*

⁴*And when he had apprehended him, he
put him in prison, and delivered him to four
quaternions of soldiers to keep him; intending
after Easter to bring him forth to the people.*

⁵*Peter therefore was kept in prison: but
prayer was made without ceasing of the
church unto God for him.*

⁶*And when Herod would have brought
him forth, the same night Peter was sleeping
between two soldiers, bound with two chains:
and the keepers before the door kept the
prison.*

⁷*And, behold, the angel of the Lord came
upon him, and a light shined in the prison:
and he smote Peter on the side, and raised
him up, saying, Arise up quickly. And his
chains fell off from his hands.*

*⁸And the angel said unto him, Gird thyself, and bind on thy sandals. And so he did. And he saith unto him, Cast thy garment about thee, and follow me.*

*⁹And he went out, and followed him; and wist not that it was true which was done by the angel; but thought he saw a vision.*

*¹⁰When they were past the first and the second ward, they came unto the iron gate that leadeth unto the city; which opened to them of his own accord: and they went out, and passed on through one street; and forthwith the angel departed from him.*

*¹¹And when Peter was come to himself, he said, Now I know of a surety, that the LORD hath sent his angel, and hath delivered me out of the hand of Herod, and from all the expectation of the people of the Jews.*

*¹²And when he had considered the thing, he came to the house of Mary the mother of John, whose surname was Mark; where many were gathered together praying.*

*¹³And as Peter knocked at the door of the gate, a damsel came to hearken, named Rhoda.*

*[14]And when she knew Peter's voice, she opened not the gate for gladness, but ran in, and told how Peter stood before the gate.*

*[15]And they said unto her, Thou art mad. But she constantly affirmed that it was even so. Then said they, It is his angel.*

*[16]But Peter continued knocking: and when they had opened the door, and saw him, they were astonished.*

In order for us to get a clear perception of what this text is conveying we must focus on why Peter was thrown into prison. During this era of the church, many believers were under persecution because of the impact of their witness. As they shared the Word of God with boldness, lives were being transformed and many were coming to Christ. For this reason, King Herod killed James the brother of John, and also had plans to kill Peter. It is important to note, that the King Herod that is referred to here is the grandson of "Herod the Great." But his plan to kill Peter was preempted through the prayers of the Church. Our finite minds cannot comprehend why God would allow James to die, but would rescue Peter. God had a plan for Peter, and as we can see in the text, His plan transcended the plans of the enemy. The Word of God says *"No weapon that is formed against us is going to prosper..."* (Isaiah 54:17).

King Herod's plan did not prosper because the church came together and prayed for Peter without ceasing. The Word of God instructs us to *"Pray without ceasing."* (1 Thess. 5:17). This means that prayer should be continuous in our every day lives. What was the assignment of the church? It was to come together corporately and pray for Peter's release from prison and simultaneously come against the forces of darkness that held him captive. In this case, it was King Herod who was being used by Satan to destroy him. We know that the devil comes with a threefold purpose: to kill, steal, and destroy (John 10:10). However, we must remember that Jesus came to destroy the works of the devil. For the Scripture says: *"...For this purpose the Son of God was manifested, that he might destroy the works of the devil (1 John 3:8).*

Webster defines the word "assignment" as *"the specific task given to you to carry out."* Therefore, the assignment of Kingdom intercessors is:

- *To pray God's will and Kingdom to come into the earth* – Matthew 6:10

- *To prevail against the Kingdom of darkness that opposes the will of God* – Ephesians 6:12

I have participated in several prayer gatherings where the prayer leaders started off with a prayer focus, but deviated from that focus to go and lay hands on someone and start a deliverance service. When this occurs, the assignment has now shifted from corporate prayer to a deliverance service. I call this a move of "flaky intercession." This happens when we began to yield to our flesh and not the Holy Spirit. Wherever there is a manifestation of the flesh, there will be confusion. We know that God is not the author of confusion. When Kingdom intercessors come together in corporate prayer, a key ingredient that must be evident is "unity." The Word says in Psalms 133:1-3:

> *Behold, how good and how pleasant it is for brethren to dwell together in unity! ²It is like the precious ointment upon the head, that ran down upon the beard, even Aaron's beard: that went down to the skirts of his garments;*
>
> *³As the dew of Hermon, and as the dew that descended upon the mountains of Zion: for there the LORD commanded the blessing, even life for evermore.*

Unity is the place where God will command the blessing. Kingdom intercessors know how to submit to one another and expose any and all manifestations of the flesh. As the church came together and prayed for Peter, God immediately responded to their intercession. The Word declares that, *"...The effectual, fervent, prayer of the righteous avails much"* (James 5:16).

As we continue to move forward in this apostolic prophetic age, we will witness more Kingdom intercessors being mobilized in our churches, cities, and nations. Kingdom intercessors are cognizant of their assignment as they attend Sunday services. They are committed to providing a prayer shield for their leaders and congregation.

Beloved, you must understand that the Kingdom of God is progressive; therefore, we can no longer be passive towards the Kingdom agenda. We must be aggressive in taking the Kingdom! We must make advancing the Kingdom our highest priority as we are instructed to do in Matthew 6:33: *"But seek first the Kingdom of God and His righteousness, and all these things shall be added to you."*

*~As Kingdom intercessors yield to the
ministry of The Holy Spirit, they tap into
dimensions of intercession that bring the
fullness of God's Glory and release a
manifestation of His will to the earth.~*

## Chapter 5

# FIVE DIMENSIONS OF INTERCESSION

As a young woman graduating from high school, I had many career aspirations. Circumstances, however, led me to enlist in the Army National Guard. It was a time of great personal growth for me as I met and trained with people from a variety of cultures and backgrounds that I had never experienced. Growing up in a community within the city of Little Rock, Arkansas, African Americans and Caucasians were the only two cultures that I had encountered. However, in this new environment, another dimension of social and cultural interaction was opened up to me.

During the time when I enlisted, they were starting a new program where the men and women trained together. This was referred to as *"co-ed training."* Most everyone that I met was under 25 years of age, scared, and not knowing what to expect. If you are familiar with the movie *An Officer and a Gentlemen*, you have an idea about how our first day went.

The next day we had to go through the obstacle course. The course was a physical and mental challenge. We learned our strengths and weaknesses and were challenged to diversify our capabilities. The overall objective of the course was to build confidence, teamwork, and to learn how to fight under pressure. One lesson I learned was that my enemy also had a strategy – one which I could not underestimate. The strategies and principles that I learned in the Army were implemented in my every day life. The overall purpose of basic training was clear: They wanted the soldiers to be skilled, trained and ready to engage in combat.

I believe that God is raising up an army, composed of believers whom He will use to advance His Kingdom as they utilize the weapons of prayer and intercession. His generals are equipping and empowering them, instructing them in the many dimensions of intercession.

I have learned through my experiences in intercession that there are different types of intercessors who have been given a special anointing to flow in different dimensions according to their level of training and gifting. As I stated in the introduction to this book, the type of intercessors that are emerging in this hour are skilled and trained elite troops. They are Kingdom minded, militant, and radical. They understand and know how to utilize the gifts of the Spirit as they flow in these different dimensions. Many of them have an apostolic and prophetic mandate.

In this chapter we will identify five dimensions of intercession into which the Lord has given me insight. Some of you may already have revelation and flow in some or all of these different types of intercession. Nevertheless, the more understanding that we have of these different areas, the more effective we will be at maneuvering in them as we advance God's Kingdom. The Bible says *"...in all thy getting, get understanding"* (Proverbs 4:7). It is imperative that we gain spiritual understanding and fresh insight into these different types of intercession so that we can flow skillfully in them.

I pray that you open your mind and spirit to what God is going to impart into you through this chapter. I prophesy that as you yield to what the Spirit of the Lord is saying in the following paragraphs, you will move into new and greater depths of intercession.

### *Strategic Intercession*

As Kingdom intercessors take dominion in the earth realm, they do so by divine strategies that God is releasing. Webster's dictionary defines "strategy" as *"a plan of action."* Therefore, one definition of strategic intercession is a group of believers coming together with a plan of action on behalf of a person, people, place, or circumstance, which desperately needs God's intervention.

I had the opportunity to attend a corporate prayer gathering in Garland, Texas. Many of the leaders are uniting in corporate prayer every Saturday at different church locations in that region. They are bringing their strategies together to effectively bring Kingdom transformation in that region. As they come together in one spirit and one purpose, God reveals to them the strongholds that are hovering over the region. These are Kingdom minded people who understand that no one person, group, or entity can conquer a city. They come together in unity, and implement strategic intercession and spiritual warfare.

In order for you to take a region, you must eradicate the ruling spirit over that region. The ruling spirits are called territorial spirits. They influence people and a community in a geographical area. These territorial spirits are a part of Satan's hierarchy described in Ephesians 6:12: *"For we wrestle not against flesh and blood, but against principalities, against powers, against the rulers of the darkness of this world, against spiritual wickedness in high places."*

As we observe our enemy's hierarchy, we must also perceive that Satan operates by blinding the minds of unbelievers in a region so they cannot perceive the truth. The Scripture says in 2 Corinthians 4:3-4: *"But if our gospel be hid, it is hid to them that are lost: In whom the god of this world hath blinded the minds of them which believe not, lest the light of the glorious gospel of Christ, who is the image of God, should shine unto them."*

Strategic intercession pursues the heart of God. We know that God is concerned about souls. Strategic intercession eradicates the power of darkness, so that a lost and dying humanity can see the light of the gospel. I believe that when God assigns you to a region and gives you spiritual authority over it, He also gives you the anointing and grace to influence and take that region for the Kingdom of God. I have seen many of the five-fold ministry gifts attempting to minister in regions where it is evident that they have not been given an anointing or grace. It is clear that God has not assigned or appointed them to that region. In other words, they are in a region without a mandate for that region. They are not fruitful because God did not call them there.

As Kingdom intercessors come together corporately to implement strategic intercession, there are key components that they utilize in advancing the Kingdom. Here are some components of strategic intercession:

- Binding and loosing (Matthew 16:18)
- Identifying territorial strongholds in a region (2 Corinthians 10:4)

- Spiritual mapping
- Prayer Walking

Each of these components is needed if we are going to transform a community, region, or nation.

One passage of Scripture that gives a vivid picture of a territorial spirit is found in Daniel 10:13, which reads: *"But the prince of the kingdom of Persia withstood me one and twenty days: but, lo, Michael, one of the chief princes, came to help me; and I remained there with the kings of Persia."*

In this passage of Scripture, Daniel is engaged in spiritual warfare, the battle that exists between the powers of darkness and the Kingdom of God. The prince of Persia was a fallen angel assigned to Persia, a regional entity. In the previous chapter, we find Daniel praying and fasting. He is seeking God concerning Jeremiah's prophecy regarding the desolation of Jerusalem that would last for seventy years. As he fasted and waited on the Lord, God showed him a vision (Chapter 10) about which he inquires of the Lord for understanding.

Note that God heard Daniel when he had offered up his prayer on the first day. However, the angel that was responding to the words spoken by Daniel was held up by a demonic force that delayed the answer to his prayer (v. 4). According to the Word, when the righteous cry, God hears (Psalms 34:17). There may be times when our prayers are delayed, but beloved, know that they will not be denied! Although Daniel's prayer was heard the first day, he did not receive the answer to that prayer until 21 days later!

Also, we want to perceive the way God responds to our prayers. He responds with "yes," "no," and "wait." I encourage you not to lose hope for what God has promised to you. Maybe you are in waiting mode right now, believing God for a request that you have presented. It's not something crazy, but your request is in line with the Word of God. Daniel had to wait for 21 days.

I am waiting right now for God to bless me with my husband. I gave the Lord this request at the age of 29. I am now 53 years old. Someone once asked me a question, "Are you sure it is God's will for you to get married?" I responded with a "yes." How did I know that it is God's will? Well, the Word of God makes it clear in the book of Genesis, chapter two, where God said that it is not good for man to be alone. When he made that statement to Adam, He later created a help meet for him, whom we know as Eve. The desire to be married was given to men and women by God.

The Word declares that He will give me the desires of my heart as I delight in Him. Also, in case you have not noticed, God is raising up teams in this hour. The Word said that one could chase a thousand to flight, but two ten thousand! It is clear from this Scripture that two are more powerful than one. Yes beloved, I too am in my waiting mode, and I will continue to wait until my "Boaz" manifests!

Now, as we read Daniel 10 in its entirety, we will notice that God sent two angels to Daniel. One angel came as a messenger to inform Daniel that His prayer had been heard and received. Some theologians believe that the angel that appeared was Christ. However, others dispute this theory, because Christ would not need the assistance of an angel to demolish the Prince of Persia.

The other angel is specifically identified as "Michael," one of the chief princes or warring angels that came to overthrow the Prince of Persia. Michael was an authorized agent from heaven sent to earth to protect Israel. We must understand the ministry of angels and how they play a vital role in bringing our prayers into full manifestation. As we just saw in Daniel's case, angels respond to not just any words, but to the Word of God. That's why it is imperative that we pray according to the Word of God. This is how we activate angels.

In strategic intercession, we act as God's authorized agents, enforcing His will in this earthly sphere. We receive the burden of the Lord and pray it through. This requires consistency and perseverance until we see a manifestation!

### *Prophetic Intercession*

We are living in a time when true apostolic and prophetic ministries are emerging around the globe. However, I believe that we use the word "prophetic" too loosely. Ephesians 4:11 identify the apostolic and prophetic as being valid offices among the five-fold ministry gifts, and these two terms are very popular in this hour. But while many are lining up to place one of these titles in front of their names, I have found that a lot of the believers who say they are Prophets do not have a clear understanding of the "prophetic."

I have witnessed people standing up to share their testimony of how God called them to the pathetic ministry, the prosthetic ministry, and so on. I believe that if you feel that God has called you to the Prophetic Ministry, you should at least know how to pronounce the word and define it. Unfortunately, a lot of believers have little or no understanding of the prophetic.

Any believer can flow in the prophetic. However, that does not necessarily mean that you are a Prophet. Every Spirit filled believer has the ability to prophesy. Like all the gifts, we release the gift of prophecy by faith. Paul admonishes us in the Scriptures to "covet to prophesy" in 1 Corinthians 14:39. The Greek word for prophesy in this text is "propheteia" *prof-ate-yoo-o*, which means *"to foretell events, speak under inspiration, or to exercise the Prophetic office."*

When we prophesy, it is by illumination of the Holy Spirit, causing us to bring forth divine utterance. When we flow in the prophetic, we are speaking forth the mind and counsel of God. We don't know the mind of God. However, according to 1 Corinthians 2:11, the Holy Spirit does: *"For what man knoweth the things of a man, save the spirit of man which is in him? even so the things of God knoweth no man, but the Spirit of God."*

When God reveals something to you about a situation that you know nothing about in your own understanding, or gives you specific direction for the purpose of prayer, it is called "prophetic intercession. God said in Amos 3:7 *"Surely the Lord God will do nothing, except He reveals His secrets to His servants the prophets."* When God wants to manifest His purpose in the earth, He looks for a man or woman. As the prophetic intercessor yields to what God has revealed, he or she begins to speak forth the promises of God.

God has many channels through which He communicates to His people. Oftentimes, He will speak to the prophetic intercessor through dreams and visions. God spoke this way to many of the prophets in the Old Testament. As you flow in this dimension of intercession, you must be able to recognize the voice of God. The Word of God says, *"...my sheep hear my voice and I know them and they follow me..."* (John 10:27). However, there are factors that deter the prophetic intercessor from hearing God:

- Unresolved issues in the heart – Psalms 51

- Not spending quality time in God's presence

- Failure to study the Word of God – 2 Tim 2:15

Prophetic intercessors are also watchmen. God gives them the ability to see beyond the natural realm. God conveyed to Ezekiel the duty of the watchmen in this passage of Scripture:

> *Again the word of the LORD came unto me, saying, ²Son of man, speak to the children of thy people, and say unto them, When I bring the sword upon a land, if the people of the land take a man of their coasts, and set him for their watchman: ³If when he seeth the sword come upon the land, he blow the trumpet, and warn the people;*

> *⁴Then whosoever heareth the sound of the trumpet, and taketh not warning; if the sword come, and take him away, his blood shall be upon his own head.*

> *⁵He heard the sound of the trumpet, and took not warning; his blood shall be upon him. But he that taketh warning shall deliver his soul.*

*⁶But if the watchman see the sword come,
and blow not the trumpet, and the people be
not warned; if the sword come, and take any
person from among them, he is taken away in
his iniquity; but his blood will I require at the
watchman's hand.*

*⁷So thou, O son of man, I have set thee a
watchman unto the house of Israel; therefore
thou shalt hear the word at my mouth, and
warn them from me.*

*⁸When I say unto the wicked, O wicked
man, thou shalt surely die; if thou dost not
speak to warn the wicked from his way, that
wicked man shall die in his iniquity; but his
blood will I require at thine hand.*

*⁹Nevertheless, if thou warn the wicked of
his way to turn from it; if he do not turn from
his way, he shall die in his iniquity; but thou
hast delivered thy soul. (Ezekiel 33:1-9)*

According to the above passage of Scripture,
the primary responsibility of the watchman was to
warn the people of approaching enemies. When the
prophetic intercessors flow in the seer anointing, they
are able to recognize demonic forces that try to come
into the church, a region, or territory.

I remember serving as head intercessor at a local
church in Houston, Texas. It was an apostolic house

and the head watchman was one of the intercessors on the prayer team. She had a keen eye. I would even say she had an eagle eye. God had anointed her to see the enemy when he came into the house. God would use her to expose the plan of the enemy manifesting through individuals before they could bring division in the house. This is the assignment of the watchmen. If the watchmen failed to warn the leader or people they would be held accountable to God. Sometimes as prophetic intercessors our assignment can be challenging. Nevertheless, we must obey God and remain faithful to the assignment.

## *Warfare Intercession*

Earlier in this chapter we talked about the hierarchy of the enemy that was revealed to us in Ephesians 6:10. Paul stated that we wrestle not against flesh and blood. Webster's dictionary defines the word "wrestle" as *"combat, to overcome an opposing tendency or force."*

I remember going to a wrestling match with my father as a child. As the two wrestlers came together, one thing that stood out was their facial expressions. They approached each other with a demeanor that was vigilant. The message that each wrestler was conveying with their body language was, "You are going down,"

Warfare intercession is a dimension of intercession where you combat your enemy with prophetic

movements or acts. When you move into this dimension of prayer, you are moving with a warrior's
mentality. A warrior is someone engaged in or experienced in warfare. In 2 Corinthians 10:4, the word
"warfare" is translated from the Greek word *"stra-
teia,"* meaning *"apostolic career."* It is imperative
that you understand that this is not a physical fight.
The Bible instructs us to fight the good fight of faith.
Faith is both a defensive and offensive weapon that
we utilize in warfare. You must understand that it is
your faith that the enemy is after.

David, a man's after God's own heart, was also
a mighty warrior. He was taught by the Lord how
to be effective in warfare. The Scripture says in
Psalm 144:1-2 : *"Praise be to the LORD my Rock,
who trains my hands for war, my fingers for battle.
He is my loving God and my fortress, my stronghold
and my deliverer, my shield, in whom I take refuge,
who subdues peoples under me."* God revealed
to David a strategy on how he was to maneuver in
warfare against his enemy Goliath. He implemented
the strategy that God gave him and is now known as
a mighty warrior because, among his many valiant
deeds, he slew the giant.

As you shift into this dimension of intercession,
your prayer language shifts into an authoritative
mode. You began to pray with authority and power.

Warfare intercessors understand their position in
Christ. The Bible declares that we have been made

to sit *"...in heavenly places with Christ Jesus."* (Ephesians 2:6). The King of Kings and Lord of Lords is seated on the throne and we are allowed to sit with Him. It is imperative to note that we are engaging in two dimensions in warfare. One realm is visible, and one is invisible. For the Word says: *"While we look not at the things which are seen, but at the things which are not seen: for the things which are seen are temporal; but the things which are not seen are eternal."* (2 Corinthians 4:18).

Nevertheless, our focus is on what's eternal, and we know that the Word of God endures forever. I have been a participant in prayer gatherings where God used warfare intercessors to corporately pull down the strongholds of the enemy in individual lives and territories. Also, there have been assignments that my team and I have received from the Lord, where we go into territories and conduct research to obtain information related to the person, community, or nation that was the target of our intercession. Implementing this strategy made us more effective in warfare. The Bible instructs us to not be ignorant of Satan's devices (2 Corinthians 2:11).

I want to share some of the manifestations of the Spirit that I have experienced in warfare intercession:

1. *The sword of the Lord* – The Sword is symbolic of the Word of God. I visualize the Word of God as a mighty Sword in my hand, and I raise up the

Sword and cut up every assignment of the enemy over the request that I am warring over. I also root out every spirit that God reveals to me that may be holding an individual or territory captive.

2. *The movement of the feet* – As I move my feet and pray in the Spirit, I am taking territories for the Kingdom of God to be advanced

3. *Clapping of the hands* –As I clap my hands, demonic forces flee and there is great breakthrough for those who are in captivity

4. *Roar of the lion* – This mighty roar announces that the Kingdom of God is here.

As we maneuver in this dimension of intercession, we must be reminded that all that we do must be done decently and in order. We must remember that the battle is not ours but the Lord's, so don't attempt to engage in warfare alone. You must stay connected to the Body of Christ as we draw strength from one another.

### *Corporate Intercession*

Corporate intercession is probably one of the most misunderstood forms of prayer we find described in the Bible. Usually when Christians get together to pray, a whole array of prayers are offered by each individual instead of the group simply bringing a few focused prayers in complete unity before the Lord.

Corporate intercession is when Kingdom intercessors come together united, exercising their faith, and pray through a specific prayer assignment from the Lord. The word "corporate," means combined into one. Therefore, corporate intercession brings every culture in the Kingdom together as one. This was Jesus cry for the Church in John 17. He reiterated several times, "Lord make them one." The call to corporate intercession comes from 2 Chronicles 7:14 which says: *"If my people, which are called by my name, shall humble themselves, and pray, and seek my face, and turn from their wicked ways; then will I hear from heaven, and will forgive their sin, and will heal their land."*

This is a call for the Church, God's family, to come together in a spirit of humility and seek the face of God. When we seek the face of God, He reveals to us our assignment of intercession, including who and what we are to pray for. As we meet the conditions in this passage of Scripture, God promises to heal our land. The early Church understood the significance of corporate prayer as they came together in the Upper Room. The Scripture reveals to us in Acts 1:14: *"These all continued with one accord in prayer and supplication, with the women, and Mary the mother of Jesus, and with his brethren."*

Today, corporate prayer is probably one of the most neglected functions of the Church. I believe this is because of a lack of teaching on this type of prayer. Most believers know how to come to church and pray individually, but not corporately. Most of our corporate prayer gatherings usually have fewer in attendance than other church functions. The response is greater for a gospel musical, the "Preaching Bowl," or "100 women in white," than a corporate prayer gathering. The enemy attempts to obstruct these gatherings, because he knows the power that is released as a result of the Church coming together in unity. It is important for us to understand that when we come together to pray corporately, it is for Kingdom purposes. Following are some of those purposes.

- To come together in unity and agreement and ask God to fulfill specific prayer request – Philippians 4:6

- To encourage repentance - Romans 10: 1-4

- To avert the judgment of God over nations - Numbers 14:11-21

- To ensure deliverance - 1 Samuel 7:5-9

- To give blessings – Number 6: 23-27

I can attest that communities and nations have been transformed as a result of corporate intercession. This book was born out of a desire to learn how to pray which resulted from the effectiveness of corporate prayer gatherings that I had attended and hosted.

I remember the first corporate prayer that I participated in when I relocated to Houston, Texas in 1994. Members of a local church came together and prayed. There were no instructions given. Everyone prayed at different locations. Some prayed at the altar, some at the back, and some on the wall. Some prayed in their prayer language, others prayed with understanding. When we finished praying, we left and went to our separate destinations. I thought to myself, 'This is not corporate prayer.'

That's why I can appreciate ministries like Eddie and Alice Smith Ministries, where I gained fresh insight and revelation related to corporate intercession. Eddie and Alice are the founders of the U.S. Prayer Center in Houston, Texas. They have authored several books on prayer, intercession, and deliverance.

I had the opportunity to attend one of their corporate prayer gatherings many years ago. I knew that the Lord led me there. I observed how Alice gave the instructions and shared some prayer points on how we were to flow. Eddie was the worship leader who ushered us into the presence of God. The atmosphere was conducive for us to move into intercession because we were in the presence of God. Alice called me up and gave me the microphone and I began to pray out of the heart of God. I was glad the Lord led me there. It was if the Lord was saying to me, "This is how corporate prayer should flow!"

I began to go to other corporate prayer gatherings in Houston, Texas. As the Lord began to open doors for me in different regions to go and teach the workshop, "Lord Teach Me How to Pray," I would take the guidelines that Eddie and Alice produced. They have guidelines for leaders entitled *10 Guidelines for Leaders of Corporate Intercession*, and guidelines for participants entitled, *15 Guidelines for Participants in Corporate Intercession*. They also have a teaching on corporate prayer on video. If you are a prayer leader in a church or ministry, these are excellent resources to help you with corporate intercession. You can obtain more information on Eddie and Alice by going to their website: www.usprayercenter.org.

## Apostolic Intercession

As we see a manifestation of the five-fold ministry gifts coming together, we can attest that we are living in an apostolic and prophetic age. The fulfillment of Old Testament prophecy requires the apostles and prophets to be restored back to the church. If the Church is going to be the glorious church that Jesus shall return for, these two offices can no longer be neglected. C. Peter Wagner states "*I believe that the government of the church is finally coming into place, as the Scripture teaches in Eph. 2, with the founda-*

*tion of the church being the apostles and prophets."* The apostolic movement of the church is a progressive and miraculous movement.

In order for us to understand apostolic intercession, we must first define the term "apostolic." In his book *Apostolic Dictionary*, John Eckhardt defines "apostolic" as *"the adjective that describes the characteristics of an apostle."* An apostle is somebody who has been sent. The Greek word is *'apostolos,'* which means, *"One who is sent."* It relates to a person who has been given a commission. They have been set apart for the cause of the gospel (Romans 1:1). As we look in the New Testament we will find some of the characteristics of an apostle. An apostle is one who:

- Plants churches 1 Corinthians 3:10-11 (Galatians 1:6-10, 3:13).

- Takes the gospel to un-reached places (Romans 15:20).

- Appoints and trains leaders (Acts 14:21-23 and Titus 1:5).

- Deals with doctrinal problems and sin (1 Corinthians 1:1-16:24 and Acts 15).

- Networks churches and promotes unity (1 Corinthians 16:1-4, Ephesians 4:1-16, Romans 15:25-27).

"Apostolic" and "Governmental Intercession" are terms that are used interchangeably and are basically the same. Apostolic intercession deals with governmental jurisdiction over nations or territories. The apostolic intercessor make proclamations, declarations, and decrees over a people, region, or nation, with the objective being to unlock God's Kingdom purposes in the earth. Their apostolic prayers eradicate religious systems and structures to pave the way for the message of the Kingdom to be presented in a region. Their mandate is to see the Kingdom of God invade every area of our society. The Word declares in Revelation 11:15: *"And the seventh angel sounded; and there were great voices in heaven, saying, The kingdoms of this world are become the kingdoms of our Lord, and of his Christ; and he shall reign for ever and ever."*

Therefore, the apostolic intercessor flows in a breaker anointing. They eradicate barriers that deter the message of the Kingdom from coming forth. Several barriers have deterred the Church of today. Some of theses barriers are:

- Religion and tradition
- Denominationalism
- Doctrines of men
- Culture
- Racism and Prejudice

Because these barriers exist in the Church, many of God's people all over the world do not have a clear understanding of the Kingdom. It is not being conveyed in many of our churches.

Sometime ago, I received an assignment from the Lord to have a corporate prayer gathering in Little Rock, Arkansas. As I received this assignment, I could immediately identify with Jonah! However, I did not make a detour to another city. I knew that I had to obey God. I was reluctant to go to this city, because I grew up there and remembered the depth of prejudice and racism that existed there. There were other territorial spirits that ruled that region as well. Nevertheless, I was determined that I was not going to allow any of my past experiences deter me from my assignment.

The Christian community consisted of predominately traditional Baptist churches. I knew that this assignment was going to be challenging, so I inquired of the Lord for a strategy. I sent out letters to pastors in the region, asking them if they would be available to meet with me. I shared the vision that the Lord had given and how it was imperative for leaders in the region to unite. With the few who responded, we came together and coordinated a team for the corporate prayer gathering. I remembered the word by Chuck Pierce of Glory of Zion Ministries that God gave to the state of Arkansas. I took this word with me as the Lord said we needed to revisit it. I reminded the people that because this was a prophetic word, it would be fulfilled. The Lord also gave me a prayer for Arkansas and it was printed out and given to the

137

people who assembled at the gathering. Many leaders in that region are catching the vision of corporate prayer and repentance. It will take the Body of Christ as a whole, to change a region. As I stated earlier in this book, no one entity can effectively take a region. Today, God is raising up more apostolic ministries in order to bring reformation to people groups, cities, regions, and nations. Our prayers and intercession continues in the state of Arkansas; Lord let your will be done and your kingdom come!

*~Our nation has become prey to a
stronghold that has captivated the belly
of many believers. Fasting is the key
to overcoming the "Belly God," and a
discipline that must be restored to the Body
of Christ. ~*

## Chapter 6

# OVERCOMING THE "BELLY GOD"

Among the seven "deadly sins" recognized in
society and brought out in literature, is gluttony. The United States is known around the world
to be a country of fat people. Gluttony has become
a serious issue in our nation. Why? Because we love
to eat!

In this country, we have allowed "the belly god"
to consume us. Many of us are very familiar with
this statement: "The quickest way to a man's heart
is through his stomach." Unfortunately, I have seen
many relationships that survive only because the
wife knows how to cook a good meal!

As a result of overeating, many of Americans are faced with severe medical conditions, causing their lives to be terminated prematurely. If we are going to fulfill our destiny and complete every assignment the Lord has given us, the church must return back to the discipline of fasting. Unfortunately, many believers have become prey to the "belly god" and have accepted a lie from the enemy as it relates to fasting. Many have missed their divine appointment with God, because they refuse to fast. Let's observe Webster's definition of "belly god": *one whose great pleasure is to satisfy his appetite; a glutton.*

When we indulge in overeating, we open up the door to become a slave to the "belly god." In this chapter, we will share insight and Biblical principles related to fasting. We will see that fasting must become a way of life if we are going to be vigilant in taking territory for God's Kingdom, and living a victorious life. We will discuss different types of fasts, how Jesus expects us to fast, and how He demonstrated this discipline in His own ministry. I believe that true intercession involves not only prayer but is often times accompanied by fasting.

### What is Fasting?

Let's first look at two definitions of fasting:

**Webster's definition:** *"To abstain from all or certain foods, to eat very little or nothing."*

**Biblical definition:** The word "fast" is translated from the Hebrew word *"tsum"* (Strong's Concordance number 6684), and it means *"to abstain from food."*

The Greek word is *"nēstis"* (3523), and it means *"not eating or hungry."*

Fasting is a powerful weapon that we utilize in spiritual warfare. It is imperative that we do not confuse the concept of fasting with that of dieting. When we diet we are attempting to obtain a goal that is self-gratifying. Our focus is on weight-loss. When we fast it should be for a spiritual purpose. Consequently, when you attempt a fast you should ask yourself this question: What is my motive for fasting? Let's look at some reasons to fast:

- To draw closer to God, so that I can hear his voice

- To gain spiritual insight and understanding concerning a situation

- To crucify fleshly appetites

- To overcome temptation

- To break off spiritual bondages

Fasting has been used in nearly every religion in the world, including Christianity, Judaism,

Buddhism, and Islam. In some countries it is used as a medical therapy for many conditions. We will find several examples of fasting in the Old and New Testaments. Fasting is a physical and spiritual discipline that should be exercised in the Church today.

### *Fasting as Demonstrated by Jesus and the Prophets*

I believe that in everything Jesus requires us to do, He leads by example. While the Church debates whether or not fasting is a command, it is clear that it is a discipline that Jesus requires from us. Jesus gives the disciples this directive in Matthew 6:17-18: *"But thou, when thou fastest, anoint thine head, and wash thy face; That thou appear not unto men to fast, but unto thy Father which is in secret: and thy Father, which seeth in secret, shall reward thee openly."*

In this passage of Scripture, Jesus gives us instructions on how we are to fast, and indicates that our fasting should be unto the Lord. In layman's terms, when you fast, you do not have to make a public announcement, or look like you are fasting. I remember a friend of mine who would go on a fast and the whole church would be cognizant of it. When she went to work, she would tell all of her co-workers that she was on a fast, and for those among them who were not familiar with the terminology, of course she would define it! She would always have a big black Bible sitting on her desk, and she would never participate in employee luncheons.

142

This type of behavior was evident when the Pharisees fasted. But Jesus condemns this type of behavior when fasting, because it is self righteous. God is not glorified through self exaltation. Rather, we should humble ourselves before God when we implement a fast. The Bible says that Jesus was led into the wilderness by the Holy Spirit. Let's look at a very familiar passage of Scripture referred to as "*the temptation of Jesus*," found in Matthew 4:1-11:

> *Then was Jesus led up of the Spirit into the wilderness to be tempted of the devil.*
>
> *²And when he had fasted forty days and forty nights, he was afterward an hungred.*
>
> *³And when the tempter came to him, he said, If thou be the Son of God, command that these stones be made bread.*
>
> *⁴But he answered and said, It is written, Man shall not live by bread alone, but by every word that proceedeth out of the mouth of God.*
>
> *⁵Then the devil taketh him up into the holy city, and setteth him on a pinnacle of the temple,*
>
> *⁶And saith unto him, If thou be the Son of God, cast thyself down: for it is written, He shall give his angels charge concerning*

*thee: and in their hands they shall bear thee up, lest at any time thou dash thy foot against a stone.*

*[7]Jesus said unto him, It is written again, Thou shalt not tempt the Lord thy God.*

*[8]Again, the devil taketh him up into an exceeding high mountain, and sheweth him all the kingdoms of the world, and the glory of them;*

*[9]And saith unto him, All these things will I give thee, if thou wilt fall down and worship me.*

*[10]Then saith Jesus unto him, Get thee hence, Satan: for it is written, Thou shalt worship the Lord thy God, and him only shalt thou serve.*

*[11]Then the devil leaveth him, and, behold, angels came and ministered unto him.*

As Jesus was ending His fast, the devil came to tempt Him. The Word says that *"Jesus was hungry."* To be hungry means to have a need for food. Oftentimes, when the appetite is not satisfied with food, hunger pangs will occur which can bring discomfort to the physical body. Nevertheless, Jesus withstood the test. Let's look at the three areas of temptation that the devil presented to Jesus:

1. *Lust of the flesh* – Considering that Jesus was hungry, the devil challenges Him to command the stones to be turned into bread.

   **Jesus response:** *Man does not live by bread alone* (Deut. 8:3).

2. *The pride of life* – The devil sets Jesus on top of the pinnacle and challenges His identity, suggesting that He throw Himself down to see whether He is truly the Son of God.

   **Jesus response:** *Thou shalt not tempt the Lord thy God* (Deut: 6:16).

3. *Lust of the eyes* – The devil takes Jesus to a high mountain and offers Him all the kingdoms of the world, if Jesus will only worship him.

   **Jesus response:** *You should worship the Lord your God, and him only shall you serve* (Deut. 6:13).

As you can see, Jesus resisted each temptation by speaking the Word of God! Therefore, prayer, accompanied by fasting and the Word of God, will give you strength and power to stand against the enemy! Jesus demonstrated through His own personal experience the power of fasting. After Jesus' temptation in the wilderness, He began His ministry. The Bible

145

declares that Jesus went forth healing the sick, and casting out demons.

There are several examples of corporate fasts in both the Old and New Testaments. One corporate fast that manifested the greatest revival in Biblical history is found in the book of Jonah:

*And the word of the LORD came unto Jonah the second time, saying, ²Arise, go unto Nineveh, that great city, and preach unto it the preaching that I bid thee. ³So Jonah arose, and went unto Nineveh, according to the word of the LORD. Now Nineveh was an exceeding great city of three days' journey. ⁴And Jonah began to enter into the city a day's journey, and he cried, and said, Yet forty days, and Nineveh shall be overthrown.*

*⁵So the people of Nineveh believed God, and proclaimed a fast, and put on sackcloth, from the greatest of them even to the least of them. ⁶For word came unto the king of Nineveh, and he arose from his throne, and he laid his robe from him, and covered him with sackcloth, and sat in ashes. ⁷And he caused it to be proclaimed and published through Nineveh by the decree of the king and his nobles, saying, Let neither man nor beast, herd nor flock, taste any thing: let them not feed, nor drink water: ⁸But let man and beast be covered with sackcloth, and cry*

146

*mightily unto God: yea, let them turn every one from his evil way, and from the violence that is in their hands. ⁹Who can tell if God will turn and repent, and turn away from his fierce anger, that we perish not? ¹⁰And God saw their works, that they turned from their evil way; and God repented of the evil, that he had said that he would do unto them; and he did it not. (Jonah 3:1-10).*

What is interesting in this text is that the King heard the warning from Jonah and obeyed the instructions to go on the fast. The King, who was the leader of that day, was able to influence the people to adhere to the instructions. As a result of the city of Nineveh coming together in corporate prayer and fasting, God saw their hearts, and did not release his anger upon them. In fact, Nineveh experienced a great revival as a result of the corporate fast!

As we observe current events in our society, we can attest that there is much chaos in our world. God is doing a shaking in our land. This is what the Lord Almighty says: *'In a little while I will once more shake the heavens and the earth, the sea and the dry land. I will shake all nations, and the desire of all nations will come, and I will fill this house with glory,' says the Lord Almighty.* (Hag 2:6-7 KJV). God is shaking in five areas:

- The earth
- The heavens

- The sea
- The dry land
- The nations

As this shaking is taking place, we will witness major catastrophes in the earth. There will be some judgments that even the prayers of the righteous will not be able to avert. God must judge the sin and lawlessness in our land. The Word says that judgment will began in the house of the Lord. Nevertheless, we will continue to fast and pray. The Word also tells us that where sin does abound, grace abounds much more (Romans 5:20).

I am reminded of a conference that I attended at Glory of Zion Ministries in Dallas, Texas. Apostle John Eckhardt was one of the speakers and his topic of discussion was on fasting. After preaching and teaching on fasting he called all of the prayer leaders to come to the altar. At that time, I was the overseer of Warfare International Ministries, Inc., and the Head Intercessor at a local church in Houston, Texas. I had the awesome responsibility to mobilize a team of intercessors in the church with corporate prayer assignments, and provide a prayer covering for the visionary and family, leadership team, congregation, and region.

I remember the Apostle saying to us that the church must get back to fasting. It was like an urgent call to fasting. As I went to the altar, I went expecting to receive an impartation from the Lord through His messenger. The impartation that I received was taken to my pastor, who imparted it into the congregation. The impartation that we received from Apostle shifted our congregation to another level in fasting. Our church was already pretty disciplined in fasting; however we had to go to the next level of fasting because of what God had promised the visionary.

We dedicated the first seven days of the month to the Lord as we came together for a corporate fast. God gave us a prayer focus through the visionary and we came together in unity and implemented the prayer focus. We saw God move in miraculous ways as the anointing intensified in the visionary, and all those who submitted to the corporate fast. We witnessed the manifestation of "suddenly" blessings. Our hunger for God and evangelism escalated. Many gifts were activated as God thrust us into new realms of His glory!

## *This Kind Comes Out Only by Prayer and Fasting*

There are some deliverance that will not manifest without prayer and fasting. Jesus makes this very clear to His disciples as they attempt to cast a demon out of a young boy in Matthew 17:21: *"Howbeit this kind goeth not out but by prayer and fasting."* However, we must read the chapter in its entirety in order to understand what Jesus truly meant in this text. In the text we have a man identified by the writer as *"...a certain man...,"* who is desperate to

149

get his son cured from being a lunatic. He brings him to Jesus' disciples who were not able to cast the devil out of his son. The disciples were distraught, and wondered why they were not able to cure the little boy. Although, the disciples had been given authority to heal, it appeared that they had not yet learned how to appropriate the power of God. Since the disciples failed to meet the need of this man, he goes to Jesus and falls at His feet requesting Him to have mercy.

Jesus in frustration tells the disciples to bring the boy to Him and he rebukes the devil, and He departed out of him, and the child was cured from that very hour (verse 18). Why was Jesus frustrated? Because of His disciples' lack of faith! The disciples questioned Jesus as to why they were unable to cast out the devil. Jesus addresses the issue of their faith. Jesus even called them a "faithless and perverse generation," although it is not clear if Jesus was rebuking the disciples or the crowd. On another occasion Jesus specifically address the unbelief in His disciples in Matthew 17:20: *"And Jesus said unto them, Because of your unbelief: for verily I say unto you, If ye have faith as a grain of mustard seed, ye shall say unto this mountain, Remove hence to yonder place; and it shall remove; and nothing shall be impossible unto you."*

It is imperative to note, that we must have these three (3) elements; faith, prayer and fasting, working simultaneously to receive this type of deliverance. The miraculous power of God was manifested, and the Scripture says that the boy was cured the moment Jesus cast out the devil. I can attest to the power of fasting in my own life. For me fasting has become a lifestyle.

I cannot imagine fulfilling my destiny or maximizing my full potential without this spiritual discipline. I developed this discipline in my early years of ministry because there was no way I could live a holy life without fasting. I shared earlier in my testimony how God delivered me from a lifestyle of sexual perversion. I now understand that my body belongs to God, and that I must glorify Him in my body.

Paul in the book of Galatians encourages us to, *"Stand fast therefore in the liberty wherewith Christ hath made us free, and be not entangled again with the yoke of bondage."* (Galatians 5:1). If we are to maintain this liberty, we must have a lifestyle of fasting. The Church has become too negligent of this discipline.

God is speaking to many of us regarding fasting in this hour. We must have an ear to hear. When was the last time you fasted? If you have to think about it, maybe it is time that you keep your appointment with God. I prophesy that a "fasting spirit" is coming upon you now! If you have never fasted, I pray that God will call you to the fast that He has chosen for you.

### *Different Types of Fasts*

Following are various types of fasts, which you may want to undertake:

*1. The supernatural fast* – This type of fast is described in Exodus 34:28: *"And he was there with the LORD forty days and forty nights; he did neither eat bread, nor drink water. And he wrote upon the tables the words of the covenant, the Ten Commandments."*

God had instructed Moses to go to Mt. Sinai where He would meet with him. He did not tell him to bring any food or water. Moses was in the presence of God, and everything that Moses needed was there, in His presence. The glory of God was revealed in the burning bush, and God gave Moses the Ten Commandments. Hunger and thirst had to cease in the presence of God! There is a generalization regarding the human body entitled the 'Rule of Threes': It says that Death can occur by three weeks without food, three days with out water, three minutes without air. It is evident that this was a supernatural fast because it transcends the laws of nature. God sustained Moses because he consumed no food or water.

*2. The partial fast* – Here, you omit a specific meal from your diet or refrain from certain types of foods. The Daniel fast is considered to be a partial fast. This concept was developed from two occasions that Daniel fasted for a specific amount of time. On

152

the first occasion, he fasted for ten days. In Daniel 1:8-14 we read:

> *But Daniel purposed in his heart that he would not defile himself with the portion of the king's meat, nor with the wine which he drank: therefore he requested of the prince of the eunuchs that he might not defile himself. ⁹Now God had brought Daniel into favour and tender love with the prince of the eunuchs. ¹⁰And the prince of the eunuchs said unto Daniel, I fear my lord the king, who hath appointed your meat and your drink: for why should he see your faces worse liking than the children which are of your sort? then shall ye make me endanger my head to the king. ¹¹Then said Daniel to Melzar, whom the prince of the eunuchs had set over Daniel, Hananiah, Mishael, and Azariah, ¹²Prove thy servants, I beseech thee, ten days; and let them give us pulse to eat, and water to drink.*
>
> *¹³Then let our countenances be looked upon before thee, and the countenance*
>
> *of the children that eat of the portion of the king's meat: and as thou seest, deal with thy servants. ¹⁴So he consented to them in this matter, and proved them ten days.*

Daniel chose not to defile himself with the kings food because the meat was most likely not prepared according to Jewish law, and it was more than likely sacrificed to idols. Although God gave Daniel favor with the Prince of the eunuchs, he made a decision not to compromise his own beliefs. Daniel and his friends were faithful to the laws of their religion in the midst of a culture that did not honor their God. The text reveals to us that as they went on this ten day fast, Daniel received much wisdom and understanding from the Lord; so much so in fact, that it changed his countenance! On another occasion, in Daniel 10:2-3, he fasted for 21 days. The Scripture reads: *"In those days I, Daniel, was mourning three full weeks. I ate no pleasant food, no meat or wine came into my mouth, nor did I anoint myself at all, till three whole weeks were fulfilled."*

Many Christians acknowledge this fast as the "Daniel Fast." During this fast, you limit your food intake to vegetables and water. The word "vegetable" in the Scripture actually includes both fruits and vegetables, as these were all allowed under the Jewish dietary laws. In the month of January you will find many Christians from around the globe coming together for a corporate fast. Many pastors encourage their congregations to undertake the Daniel 21-day fast, and have found it to be very effective. It is has been proven to be a powerful fast, yielding many breakthroughs.

**3. The Normal Fast** – The normal fast is abstaining from food only. This is the fast that Jesus undertook when He went into the wilderness. He ate no food and appears to have had only water. The reason scholars conclude that He drank water while on this fast is because the Scripture says He was hungry, but does not say He was thirsty.

**4. The Absolute 3-day fast** – In both the Old and New Testament we will find those who fasted for 3-days and consumed no food or drink. (Esther 4:15-16). Esther sent this reply to Mordecai:

> *"Go, gather together all the Jews who are in Susa, and fast for me. Do not eat or drink for three days, night or day. I and my maids will fast as you do. When this is done, I will go to the king, even though it is against the law. And if I perish, I perish."*

Paul also fasted for 3-days and consumed no food or drink (Acts 9:9).

It is imperative that you seek God's will before you go on any of the above-mentioned fasts. Also, if you decide to fast for a long length of time, you need to consult your physician. Nevertheless, your motive for fasting will always be the incentive for you receiving the desired results. Below you will find three (3) books on fasting that I would like to recommend, along with their respective authors:

- *God's Chosen Fast* – Arthur Wallis
- *Fasting for Spiritual Breakthrough* – Elmer L. Towns
- *Fasting* – Jentezen Franklin

## God's Chosen Fast

The early church recognized the need for fasting and the spiritual power that was unleashed as a result of it. In his book *God's Chosen Fast,* Arthur Wallis writes, *"Fasting is calculated to bring a note of urgency and [persistence] into our praying, and to give force to our pleas in the court of heaven."* Just like the early church, the End-Time Church also must recognize the need for not just personal fasting, but corporate fasting. The Bible says one can put a thousand to flight, but two ten thousand (Deut. 32:30).

When God's people fast with a proper Biblical motive-seeking God's face not His hand-with a broken, repentant, and contrite spirit, God will hear from heaven and heal our land, our churches, our communities, our nation and world. Fasting and prayer can bring about revival, a change in the direction of our nation and the nations of the earth, and ultimately, the fulfillment of the Great Commission.

Isaiah 58 presents both acceptable and unacceptable types of fasts. You will notice that the fast that the Jews presented to God was not acceptable. As they fasted, they magnified their acts of piety, desiring to be the focus of their fasting. They then questioned God as to why He had not responded to their fast! It was their custom to fast on the Day of Atonement, which was a day in which they afflicted their soul. They felt that they should be rewarded because of their external, visible works. Although, they fasted, the Bible tells us that sin persisted in their hearts. That's why God had to show them the type of fast that is acceptable to him.

Let's look at Isaiah 58:6: *"Is not this the fast that I have chosen? to loose the bands of wickedness, to undo the heavy burdens, and to let the oppressed go free, and that ye break every yoke?"* As I stated earlier in the chapter, when we fast, we must examine our motive for fasting. We all have the propensity to fast with wrong motives. Oftentimes when we are faced with circumstances that need God's divine intervention, most of us will go on a fast. We want God to move in a situation and we want Him to move now! However, when we fast, we should rather emphasize honoring God. The fast that is acceptable to God has the following purposes:

• To Loose the bands of wickedness

• To Undo heavy burdens (Psalms 55:2)

• To Let the oppressed go free

• To Break every yoke (Isaiah 10:27)

As we implement God's chosen fast, not only will we experience deliverance, but also those for whom we stand in the gap. God is concerned about souls and does not want any man to perish. (John 3:15). God also reveals to us in Isaiah 58:7 the fruit of the fast. In other words, fasting should prompt us to do the following:

- Feed the hungry

- Shelter the homeless

- Clothe the naked

Beloved, if you are still questioning where fasting is for you, I challenge you today to hear the words of Jesus in Mark 2: 20, *"But the days will come, when the bridegroom shall be taken away from them, and then shall they fast in those days."*

*~ There is a language that has been given to the citizens of the kingdom to communicate to the Father by supernatural means. As you consistently exercise this language it will thrust you into deeper realms of the supernatural and enrich your life spiritually~*

## Chapter 7

# THE KINGDOM LANGUAGE

One of the most helpless situations one could ever experience is to go to a foreign country and not know its language. How would you be able to communicate? You would certainly feel lost and alone.

When we are born into the Kingdom of God, we become members of the family of God and citizens of the Kingdom of God. Hence our citizenship is in Heaven. This truth is revealed in Philippians 3:20: *"But our citizenship is in heaven. And we eagerly await a Savior from there, the Lord Jesus Christ, [21]who, by the power that enables him to bring every-*

159

*thing under his control, will transform our lowly bodies so that they will be like his glorious body."*

Now that we are citizens of the Kingdom, we must know how to communicate in Kingdom vernacular. In this chapter we will gain insight into the different types of tongues that we receive when we enter into the Kingdom. We will also be challenged to move into realms of speaking in tongues that we may have never previously experienced or learned.

It is imperative that you understand how powerful this Kingdom language is, and how vital it is needed to thrust you into spiritual maturity. When we receive the gift of tongues, we receive the supernatural gift of speaking in another language that we did not learn. The Holy Spirit enables and empowers us to speak in tongues. We will also discover that when we exercise this gift it helps us to overcome our adversary throughout this Christian journey. You will receive the revelation that this language was promised by the Father and is a gift from the Holy Spirit to you. The Word of God states that *"My people are destroyed for lack of knowledge..."* (Hosea 4:6). I pray that this chapter will clarify all misconceptions about this gift, which is a controversial subject in most of today's churches.

One Sunday evening sometime ago, I was watching a very interesting episode of *60 Minutes.* My attention was drawn to this channel because they were literally doing a study on people speaking in tongues. They had Catholics, nuns, and Pentecostals who prayed in tongues, hooked up to machines. They conducted brain scans on all of them. The doctor, who was a radiologist, stated that while they were speaking in tongues there appeared to be increased activity in the brain, although, they could not explain why. It was beyond their intellectual ability to comprehend what was happening. Why? Because what was taking place in the brain was supernatural!

I can attest from my own experience of praying in tongues how my brain is illuminated! It's like getting your dead battery charged up. My memory is enhanced and I am more alert. I am bold and courageous! Unfortunately, many believers have not received this gift from God because of the erroneous teaching that they have received. It is imperative that you understand that every truth that you receive about the Kingdom must be received through revelation. We cannot understand the message of the Kingdom with a religious mind. The Word instructs us to be transformed by the renewing of our mind (Romans 12:1). In other words, Kingdom revelation cannot be received with a carnal mind.

In Mark 4:11-12, when one of Jesus disciples came to Him to inquire why He taught them in parables, He responded with these words:

> *And He said unto them, Unto you it is given to*
> *know the mystery of the kingdom of God: but*
> *unto them that are without, all these things*

*are done in parables: ¹²That seeing they may see, and not perceive; and hearing they may hear, and not understand; lest at any time they should be converted, and their sins should be forgiven them.*

When we become Born Again, we are given the ability to understand the Kingdom and its principles because the veil has been lifted from off our eyes. Now that we are in Christ, we can perceive those things that are spiritual, because the Spirit of God illuminates our mind.

### *The Promise and Purpose of Tongues*

In the beginning when God created Adam and Eve there was one language that they spoke as they communicated with each other. Although, it is not clear what language was spoken, many theologians believe that it was Hebrew, since that was the language of that era. It was the language of the Jews. Also, there was a time in Bible history where every culture spoke one language. We will find this truth in Genesis 11:1:

*And the whole earth was of one language, and of one speech.*

*²And it came to pass, as they journeyed from the east, that they found a plain in the land of Shinar; and they dwelt there.*

162

*³And they said one to another, Go to, let us make brick, and burn them thoroughly. And they had brick for stone, and slime had they for morter.*

*⁴And they said, Go to, let us build us a city and a tower, whose top may reach unto heaven; and let us make us a name, lest we be scattered abroad upon the face of the whole earth.*

*⁵And the LORD came down to see the city and the tower, which the children of men builded.*

*⁶And the LORD said, Behold, the people is one, and they have all one language; and this they begin to do: and now nothing will be restrained from them, which they have imagined to do.*

*⁷Go to, let us go down, and there confound their language, that they may not understand one another's speech.*

*⁸So the LORD scattered them abroad from thence upon the face of all the earth: and they left off to build the city.*

*⁹Therefore is the name of it called Babel; because the LORD did there confound the language of all the earth: and from thence did the LORD scatter them abroad upon the face of all the earth.*

This passage of Scripture depicts the historical story of the Tower of Babel. Not a myth, this Bible story is historically accurate. Unfortunately, man's desire for power and control which first showed itself at the "Fall", became evident when some "would-be" leaders decided to make themselves gods over all men, and then creating a great tower that reached up to the heavens where "only God can be." To put down the rebellion, God removed their ability to control others by confusing the language and speech, severing their line of communications. The opportunity to have power over all humanity was lost when the people were divided into many smaller groups, each speaking their own language and going their own way.

When we enter into the family of God through the new birth we are given the language to commune with God as originally intended before the fall. Jesus told his disciples that the promise of the Holy Spirit would manifest in their day. He said that when the Holy Spirit came that they would receive power (Acts 1:8). This power was needed if they were going to fulfill the Great Commission. We see a fulfillment of that promise in Act 2:1-4:

*And when the day of Pentecost was fully come, they were all with one accord in one place.*

*²And suddenly there came a sound from heaven as of a rushing mighty wind, and it filled all the house where they were sitting.*

*³And there appeared unto them cloven tongues like as of fire, and it sat upon each of them.*

*⁴And they were all filled with the Holy Ghost, and began to speak with other tongues, as the Spirit gave them utterance.*

The word *"tongues"* in the Greek is translated as a *"language"* (specifically an un-acquired language). When we receive the gift of tongues we receive a supernatural gift of speaking in another language that we did not learn. Jesus promises us in His Word that we will receive new tongues. The Bible declares in Mark 16:17, *"And these signs shall follow them that believe; In my name shall they cast out devils; they shall speak with new tongues"*

It is obvious that there are two types of tongues, a corporate tongue, which requires an interpretation, and a personal/prayer tongue that requires no inter-pretation. Paul gives us directives as it relates to both in 1 Corinthians 14:1-5:

*Follow after charity, and desire spiritual gifts, but rather that ye may prophesy.*

*²For he that speaketh in an unknown tongue speaketh not unto men, but unto God: for no man understandeth him; howbeit in the spirit he speaketh mysteries.*

*³But he that prophesieth speaketh unto men to edification, and exhortation, and comfort.*

*⁴He that speaketh in an unknown tongue edifieth himself; but he that prophesieth edifieth the church.*

*⁵I would that ye all spake with tongues but rather that ye prophesied: for greater is he that prophesieth than he that speaketh with tongues, except he interpret, that the church may receive edifying.*

In every scripture that references believers being filled with the Holy Spirit, they began to speak with other tongues. The tongues were the evidence that they had been filled with the Holy Spirit! Now, I am not implying that if you do not speak in tongues that you do not have the Holy Spirit. Below are verses that reference believers being filled with the Holy Spirit and afterward speaking in tongues:

- Jews at Pentecost are filled with the Spirit and speak in tongues - Acts 2:1-13.

- Gentiles receive the Spirit at Cornelius' house and speak in tongues – Acts 10:44-46.

- Ephesian Christians filled with the Spirit and speak in tongues - Acts 19:5-7.

The Apostle Paul makes a clear distinction between praying with the mind (understanding) and praying in tongues in 1 Corinthians 14:14-19:

*14For if I pray in an unknown tongue, my spirit prayeth, but my understanding is unfruitful.*

*15What is it then? I will pray with the spirit, and I will pray with the understanding also: I will sing with the spirit, and I will sing with the understanding also.*

*16Else when thou shalt bless with the spirit, how shall he that occupieth the room of the unlearned say Amen at thy giving of thanks, seeing he understandeth not what thou sayest?*

*17For thou verily givest thanks well, but the other is not edified.*

*18I thank my God, I speak with tongues more than ye all:*

*[19]Yet in the church I had rather speak five words with my understanding, that by my voice I might teach others also, than ten thousand words in an unknown tongue.*

Whether we speak in tongues or speak in languages we have learned, everything must be done decently and in order. We must have a clear perception of the purpose of tongues. If you do not understand the purpose of a thing, abuse is inevitable. The purpose of tongues is to:

- Speak mysteries to God – 1 Corinthians 14:2

- Edify the believer – 1 Corinthians 14:4

- Edify the church when interpreted – 1 Corinthians 14:5

- Use as a prayer language – 1 Corinthians 14:14

- Build our faith – Jude 20

There is no particular method followed to receive the gift of tongues or your prayer language. It is received by faith, and you exercise the language by faith. But there is one very important ingredient: You have to open your mouth and speak!

There are different teachings on what "Praying in the Spirit" actually means. Most Charismatics believe that it entails speaking in tongues. Other Christians believe that it refers to being "led by the Spirit" as you pray in your known tongue. We tend to agree with the first teaching, although we will not debate the point if you want to believe otherwise. The phrase "Praying in the Spirit," is referred to three times in Scripture:

1) 1 Corinthians 14:15 says, *"So what shall I do? I will pray with my spirit, but I will also pray with my mind; I will sing with my spirit, but I will also sing with my mind."* (NIV).

2) Ephesians 6:18 says, *"And pray in the Spirit on all occasions with all kinds of prayers and requests. With this in mind, be alert and always keep on praying for all the saints."* (NIV).

3) Jude 20 says, *"But you, dear friends, build yourselves up in your most holy faith and pray in the Holy Spirit."* (NIV).

It is clear that when you pray with your "mind," you are praying in a language that you have learned, such as English, French, Spanish, German, Chinese or one of many other languages acquired through intellectual assimilation. When these scriptures refer to praying "with my spirit," we understand that to mean "praying in tongues," since it is juxtaposed with the phrase, "with my mind" (See I Corinthians

14:15 in particular), implying that it is not the same thing. Nevertheless, whether we pray with our mind or with our spirit, our objective should always be to bring God glory. If we have any other motive, we are not truly praying!

### *Releasing the Gifts of Tongues in Intercession*

Speaking in tongues plays a vital role in intercession. As I mentioned earlier, the gifts of tongues aids us in fulfilling the Great Commission. When we release the gifts of tongues, we can intercede for nations. The Bible identifies two distinct tongues that we receive from the Spirit. They are identified as spiritual gifts in 1 Corinthians 12:8-10:

> *For to one is given the word of wisdom through the Spirit, to another the word of knowledge through the same Spirit, ⁹to another faith by the same Spirit, to another gifts of healings by the same Spirit, ¹⁰to another the working of miracles, to another prophecy, to another discerning of spirits, to another different kinds of tongues, to another the interpretation of tongues.*

This passage of Scripture reveals to us the gift of diverse tongues, and interpretation of tongues, given by the Holy Spirit. Spiritual gifts operate only when we are available to the Holy Spirit. While the gifts are supernatural both in source and operation, they require willing and obedient hearts through which they might find expression.

I remember attending a prayer gathering at my church, and one of the intercessors was praying when all of sudden she burst forth in a Chinese tongue. Well, I would not have had a problem with this if the woman was of Chinese ethnicity. However, she was African American, and by faith she was releasing the gift of diverse kinds of tongues. Remember, I stated earlier in this book that you cannot perceive the things of God with the natural mind. You must receive revelation from God through the Holy Spirit. The Lord revealed to me that the intercessor was praying for China in a Chinese tongue. The pastor interpreted the tongue into English. It is amazing what God will do through us when we yield to His Spirit.

I have a friend who is a pastor and also an intercessor. God has used her to intercede for many nations as she spoke in diverse kinds of tongues. I know many intercessors that pray in tongues but have not received the gift of interpretation of tongues.

I remember praying and asking God to release this gift to me, which He did. There have been times in corporate worship when the Holy Spirit would stir me up to speak in tongues to the Body of Christ. Someone in the congregation would come forth with the interpretation. This is the order of God. This is how Scripture instructs us to pray in public as it relates to speaking in tongues. However, I then desired to interpret the tongues that I would release in public worship. Remember the instructions that Paul gave in 1 Corinthians 14:23: *"So if the whole church comes together and everyone speaks in tongues, and some who do not understand or some unbelievers come in, will they not say that you are out of your mind?"* (NIV).

The answer to Paul's rhetorical question is yes, they will think you are out of your mind. There were even those on the day of Pentecost who thought the 120 were drunk. So if an uninformed person or unbeliever comes into our worship service and we are all singing or praying out loud in tongues at the same time what is the profit? There is none, according to Paul.

I pray that you will yield your vocal cords to the Holy Spirit and allow Him to release these vocal gifts to you. There are so many awesome manifestations of tongues that you can experience as you yield to the Holy Spirit. I want to share some of the manifestations of tongues that I have experienced as I flow in the different dimensions of prayer and intercession.

### *Tongues of Worship*

When the prophetic anointing is released there will be a manifestation of diverse kinds of tongues in worship. As you worship the Lord in Spirit and in Truth, you will reach a plateau. If you want to go higher in the spirit, your only option will be to sing

172

in tongues. God has released many songs from the throne room through my spirit during these times of deep worship. It seems at times as if angels are singing with me.

We know there is an angelic choir in Heaven. I believe that there are worship angels that assist us in worship. The Bible lets us know that David was a Psalmist. When the songs come forth in this manner, a Psalmist anointing is released. This is a true picture of the Davidic anointing, for the Scripture says: *"Now these be the last words of David. David the son of Jesse said, and the man who was raised up on high, the anointed of the God of Jacob, and the sweet psalmist of Israel, said, The Spirit of the LORD spake by me, and his word was in my tongue."* (2 Samuel 23:1-2).

I remember at one of our AHOP ("A House of Prayer" - a monthly cell group that comes together in unity for strategic prayer) gatherings, I received a word of prophecy from one of the prophets that was in the house.

The Prophet prophesied that God was releasing songs of deliverance through my worship. He stated that God was going to use me to minister songs of deliverance through the prophetic anointing. Well, as soon as the Prophet released this word, the fulfillment of the prophecy came forth. I immediately went to a young lady that was present and began singing in song Philippians 3:13-14: *"Brethren, I count not*

173

*myself to have apprehended: but this one thing I do, forgetting those things which are behind, and reaching forth unto those things which are before, I press toward the mark for the prize of the high calling of God in Christ Jesus.*

Now, I did not reiterate the Scripture verbatim, but the song was released from this passage. The woman immediately fell to her knees and began purging. The demonic forces that held her captive were fleeing. The woman was being delivered by the power of God through the worship song. Everyone began praising and worshipping the Lord, in awe of seeing the prophecy fulfilled so quickly. This was a suddenly manifestation! The Lord began to speak through the prophetic songs of deliverance and many were set-free and released into their destiny and purpose.

### Tongues of Warfare

Another manifestation of tongues that I have experienced is warfare tongues. I received a prayer request from a friend of mine who was stricken with cervical cancer. Many of us understand that sickness and diseases are a result of the fall. It was never God's will for us to be sick. When God created Adam and Eve that were afforded divine health, and when they chose to disobey God, their health was compromised. Isaiah shares a prophetic word as it relates to sickness in Isaiah 53:5: *"But he was wounded for our transgressions, he was bruised for our iniquities: the chastisement of our peace was upon him; and with his stripes we are healed.*" In the New Testament we will find Jesus healing people in every region that He went into. He did not refuse to heal anyone. The Scripture says in Matthew 4:23-24:

*And Jesus went about in all Galilee, teaching in their synagogues, and preaching the gospel of the kingdom, and healing all manner of disease and all manner of sickness among the people. And the report of him went forth into all Syria: and they brought unto him all that were sick, holden with divers diseases and torments, possessed with demons, and epileptic, and palsied; and he healed them.*

Therefore, we must understand that it is not God's will for us to be sick. As I started praying for my friend, I began to pray healing scriptures over her. Then I started praying in tongues. I noticed how my voice shifted to a commanding tone. I prayed like this for about 15 minutes. I can attest that although I prayed for 15 minutes, it seemed like an hour. I realized that I was engaged in spiritual warfare. The Lord revealed to me that the spirit of death was trying to hold this woman captive.

I received a call from another intercessor in North Carolina who had picked up the burden from the Lord to intercede for this same woman. We came in agreement as we began, praying in English. Then we began praying in tongues. We began to bind the spirit of death according to Matthew 18:18 and send the word to heal her. As we prayed, I saw a dark cloud dissipating. I knew that it was the spirit of death. We began to decree and declare that she would not die but live and declare the works of the Lord (Psalms 118:17).

I received an email from my friend a week later informing me that she was preparing for surgery, chemo, and radiation. I noticed that her faith had shifted from when I had last spoken to her. She just kept confessing that no matter what the doctor has said, she knew that she was healed. She was sharing testimonies of how God was using her to pray for people with cancer while she was in the hospital. Those whom she prayed for were being healed.

Beloved, there is a dimension, far beyond our comprehension, that you can enter into as you intercede for others. In this realm, your prayer tongues will penetrate and dispel the power of darkness. As we move out of the flesh and yield to the Spirit of God, we will be ready to engage in spiritual warfare.

I believe that these warfare tongues are weapons of mass destruction against our adversary. I pray in tongues everyday. It is a daily discipline that I implement to ensure that I walk in victory. If you have never prayed in tongues before, I would like to invite you to receive this gift. It will certainly enrich you spiritually and give you the power that is needed to live a victorious life!

*~You can become the greatest Prophet in your life. The word declares that you shall have whatever YOU say. Unleash the power of the spoken word to change your atmosphere!~*

## Chapter 8

# RELEASING PROPHETIC DECLARATIONS

In Genesis chapter one, we find the account of how God created the heavens and the earth. The first two verses read as follows: *"In the beginning God created the heaven and the earth. And the earth was without form, and void; and darkness was upon the face of the deep. And the Spirit of God moved upon the face of the waters."*

It is interesting to note that although the Spirit of the Lord was hovering over the waters, (which indicates that the presence of the Lord was there), nothing happened until God said something. The results are evident in the following verses:

- *Then God **said**, "Let there be light," **and there was light**. (Genesis 1:3).*

- *Then God **said**, "Let the waters below the heavens be gathered into one place ... **and it was so**. "(Genesis 1:9).*

- *Then God **said**, "Let there be lights in the expanse of the heavens to separate the day from the night ...**and it was so**." (Genesis 1:14, 15).*

- *Then God **said**, "Let the earth bring forth living creatures after their kind ...**and it was so**." Genesis 1:24).*

- *Then God **said**, "Behold, I have given you every plant yielding seed ...**and it was so**." (Genesis 1:29, 30).*

When God spoke, His own words came out of His mouth. Now, what I want you to understand is that you have the same power in your tongue that God does. The same Spirit moves through your breath and lungs. Your words have the power to change your environment.

The Bible declares *"Death and life are in the power of the tongue..."* (Proverbs 18:21). Yes, your speech will create a positive or negative environment for you. Many of us are familiar with the statement "sticks and stones may break my bones, but words will never hurt me." Well, I have news for you if you didn't already know it: that's just not true. Words are powerful! So powerful that when they are released over you they can either hurt you or heal you. That's why it is imperative that you do not allow negative words to come out of your mouth or be spoken over you.

As I began to mature in the Lord, a discipline that I implemented in my home was to never say the word "can't." I encouraged my children not to say that word either, because it has a negative connotation. The Bible declares that, "*I can do all things through Christ who strengthens me.*" (Phil. 4:13, NKJV).

I remember one of my pastors making this statement, "if you think you can, you can; if you think you can't, you can't." Given the fact that our thoughts will determine our words (Matt. 12:34), it is imperative that we think positively.

We must renew our minds daily with the Word of God. We must be like David and hide the Word in our heart (Psalm 119:11). If the Word is in your heart, when a circumstance arises in your life, you need to simply believe the Word of God. Regardless of outward appearances, trust what God has said. Why? I am glad you asked!

God is not man that He should lie (Num. 23:19). The Word of God is always true. Jesus said that Heaven and earth shall pass away, but the Word of God will remain forever (Matthew 13:31). When you speak the Word of God over your situation, you are making a prophetic declaration. As believers, we have been given the authority to decree the Word of God in every aspect of our lives. Job 22:28 reveals this truth: *"Thou shalt also decree a thing, and it shall be established unto thee: and the light shall shine upon thy ways."* However, we must be careful what we decree. God will only establish that which agrees with His Word. Therefore, we should only be speaking what God has already spoken.

I am reminded of the Church's "name it and claim it" era. Many believers were using this principle of proclamation to "blab it and grab it." Well, some were disappointed to find out that God is not obligated to honor every word spoken out of your mouth! He is only obligated to honor His Word. When you speak His Word, you are releasing His promises. Also, you must understand that some of the promises of God are conditional. In other words, to receive the promise, you must meet the condition. For example, God says the following words in Deuteronomy 11:26-28:

> *Behold, I set before you today a blessing and a curse: the blessing, if you obey the commandments of the LORD your God which I command you today; and the curse, if you do not obey the commandments of the LORD your God, but turn aside from the way which I command you today, to go after other gods which you have not known.* (NKJV).

It is clear from this passage of Scripture that in order for me to receive the blessings of the Lord, I must obey Him. It is my choice. I can either choose blessings or curses. The consequences will follow the choice I make, whether good or bad. Since the Word says we shall have whatever we "say," (Mark 11:23), in order for us to release the promises, it is clear that we must "speak." I must reiterate that if we are going to speak the promises of God, our minds must be renewed with the Word of God. Remember, we are a product of our thoughts. The Bible declares that *"...as a man thinketh so is he..."* (Proverbs 23:7).

Our world and destiny are shaped by our thoughts. A great scientist by the name of Ernest Holmes patterned his "Science of Mind" on the following precept:

> *Man, by thinking, can bring into his expe-*
> *rience whatsoever he desires ... from his*
> *own thinking. He can create such a strong*
> *mental atmosphere of success that its power*
> *of attraction will be irresistible. He can*
> *send his thoughts throughout the world and*
> *have them bring back to him whatever he*
> *wants. (Creative Mind and Success* by Ernest
> Holmes*).*

This principle has been implemented in the lives of productive and achieving men and women all around the globe. Christians and non-Christians alike have put this principle to work successfully for them.

### Say What God Says About You

In order for you to make prophetic declarations you must be clear on what God is saying about you in every aspect of your life. Since the Bible is the standard for Christian living, we must know the Word of God. We must learn to apply the Word of God to every situation or circumstance that manifests in our lives. Therefore, we must study the Word of God if we are going to know what God is saying about us. Paul challenges us with these words in 2 Timothy 2:15: *"Study to show thyself approved unto God, a workman that needeth not be ashamed, rightly dividing the word of truth."*

When we study the Word of God, we will have the faith that we need to move every mountain in our way. We know that faith comes by hearing and hearing the Word of God. We must also understand that we cannot only hear the Word but we must obey the Word. You will never ascertain if the Word works if you do not apply it to your life. You can no longer take someone else's word about it, you must know with certainty that the Word works! I have heard people stand up in church and testify that in the midst of their trials and tribulations, God gave them strength to climb the mountain. That's not what the Word says. Mark 11:22-24 declares:

*And Jesus answering saith unto them, Have faith in God. For verily I say unto you, That whosoever shall say unto this mountain, Be*

*thou removed, and be thou cast into the sea;
and shall not doubt in his heart, but shall
believe that those things which he saith shall
come to pass; he shall have whatsoever he
saith. Therefore I say unto you, What things
soever ye desire, when ye pray, believe that
ye receive them, and ye shall have them.*

The first thing Jesus told His disciples in the
above passage of Scripture was to have faith in God!
What does it mean to have faith in God? It means
that you believe what the Word of God says. It is
your faith in God that is going to move the mountain.
Unfortunately, many believers do not really believe
the Word of God. Most of the time, they just reiterate what they hear their leaders or others speak. I
have found out that unbelief is more prevalent in the
Church than in the world. Jesus rebuked his disciples for being "faithless" (Luke 9:37:41). When we
release our faith it activates the Word of God that we
have in our hearts. It quickens the Word in our hearts
to be released out of our mouth! Then we are able to
speak to the mountain. What mountain are you faced
with today? Speak to it! You have the power in your
mouth to change your atmosphere.

## *It's Application Time!*

I now impart prophetic declarations into your life
and prophesy that as you decree them daily, you will
see a manifestation of that which has been released in
the atmosphere. Expect a change! You are releasing

the promises of God in every area of your life. The Word declares that the promises of God are yes and AMEN!

## YOUR CHILDREN

*Blessed is (name your children) that walk not in the counsel of the ungodly, nor stand in the way of sinners, nor sit in the seat of the scornful. But (his/her/their) delight is in the law of the LORD; and in his law he meditates day and night (Psalms 1:1-2).*

*Lord according to your Word you will command your angels concerning (name your children) and guard them in all their ways (Psalms 91:11).*

*Father your Word declares that blessed is the man that fears the LORD, that delights greatly in his commandments. I decree that my seed is blessed and shall be mighty upon earth. I decree that wealth and riches shall be in his house and my righteousness endures for ever (Psalms 112:1-3).*

*I decree that the Lord will deliver (name your children) from wicked people and shall establish them and keep them from evil (2 Thess. 3:2-3).*

*I say that my (name your children) are a gift from the Lord (Psalm 127:3).*

*I decree that I train up (name your children) in the way that (he/she/they) should go, and when (he/she/they) is old (he/she/they) will not turn from it.*

*I decree that my children honor and respect me and their days shall be long on the earth (Exodus 20:12).*

## YOUR FINANCES

*I decree that I pay my tithes consistently and God opens up the window of heaven and pour me out blessings that I don't have room enough to receive (Malachi 3:10).*

*I decree that I sow bountifully and I am a cheerful giver (2 Corinthians 9:6-7).*

*I decree that God has given me the power to get wealth (Deut. 8:18).*

*I decree that because I give into the Kingdom it shall be given unto me good measure, pressed down, and shaken together, and running over, shall men give into my bosom. (Luke 6:38).*

*Father, I thank you because I obey and serve you, I will spend my days in prosperity, and my years in pleasures (Job 36:11).*

*I decree that I honor the Lord with my substance, and with the first fruits of all my increase, and my barns are filled with plenty, and my presses shall burst out with new wine (Proverbs 3:9-10).*

## YOUR HEALTH – A DISEASE FREE BODY

*I decree that I am prospering in every area of my life and walk in good health as my soul prospers (3 John 1:2).*

*Father your Word declares that you will restore health unto me, and will heal me of my wounds (Jeremiah 30:17).*

*Father your Word declares that you will bring me health and cure, and you will cure me, and will reveal unto me the abundance of peace and truth (Jeremiah 33:6).*

*I decree that your light shall break forth as the morning, and my health shall spring forth speedily; and my righteousness shall go before thee: the glory of the Lord shall be my rear guard (Isaiah 58:8).*

186

*I decree that the very God of peace sanctify me wholly; and my spirit, soul and body is preserved blameless, unto the coming of our Lord Jesus Christ (1 Thessalonians 5:23).*

*I decree that healing is one of my benefits in the Kingdom and I will bless the Lord who forgives all my iniquities and heals all my diseases (Psalms 103:2-3).*

*I decree that God's Word is life unto me and health unto all my flesh (Proverbs 4:22).*

## YOUR MARRIAGE

*I decree and declare that my spouse and I are one, and what God has joined together no man can put asunder (Mark 10:8-9).*

*I decree and declare that I love my spouse with the love of God, for love comes from God. Everyone who loves has been born of God and knows God. Whoever does not love does not know God, because God is love (1 John 4: 7-8).*

*I decree and declare that my spouse and I submit to one another out of reverence for Christ (Ephesians 5:21).*

*Father your Word declares that "Marriage is honorable among all, and the bed undefiled." I declare that my spouse and I honor you in our sexuality (Hebrew 13:4).*

*I decree and declare that my spouse and I walk in agreement and anything that we ask in the Father's name He will do (Matthew 18:19).*

## YOUR PASTOR

*I decree that God has given me a pastor after his own heart that feeds the flock with knowledge and understanding (Jeremiah 3:15).*

*I decree that my pastor makes seeking the Kingdom of God and His righteousness priority (Matthew 6:33).*

*I decree that my pastor loves God with all his/her heart, soul, mind and strength (Deuteronomy 6:5).*

*I decree that my pastor can do all things though Christ who strengths him/her (Philippians 4:13).*

*I decree that my pastor loves his wife as Jesus loves the Church and a hedge of protection surrounds him and his family.*

*I decree that my pastor abides in the secret place of the most high and under the shadow of the Almighty.*

*I decree that no weapon that forms against my pastor and his family, finances, vision, health, leadership team, ministries, business, shall prosper according to Isaiah 54:17.*

*I decree that Spirit of the Lord is upon my pastor in a great measure, the spirit of wisdom and understanding, the spirit of counsel and might, the spirit of knowledge and the fear of the Lord (Isaiah 11:2).*

*I decree that my pastor walks in holiness, integrity, humility, and is full of the love of God (Hebrews 12:14, Proverbs 11:3, James 4;6 1 John 4:7-8).*

*I decree that my pastor is a tither, cheerful giver, and bountiful sower, and practices good stewardship (Malachi 3:10, 2 Corinthians 9:6-7, 1 Timothy 6:17-19).*

*I decree that my pastor has favor with God and with men (1 Samuel 2:26).*

*I decree that my pastor enjoys an abundant life and God has chosen to give my pastor His Kingdom, and all the blessings and promises in the Kingdom belong to him. I decree every spiritual blessing in the Heavenly places to come to my pastor NOW. (John 10:10, Ephesians 1:3, 2 Peter 1:2-4).*

*I decree that the fruit of the Spirit is evident in the lives of my pastor and spouse according to Galatians 5:22.*

*I decree that my pastor has a good name and is respected in the city, community, and nation (Proverbs 22:1).*

## YOUR BUSINESS

*I decree that my God makes all grace abound toward me in every favor and earthly blessing, so that I have all sufficiency for all things and I abound to every good work, in my business (2 Corinthians 9:8).*

*I decree that I am blessed in the city, blessed in the field, blessed coming in, blessed going out, blessed in the basket and blessed in my business, blessed in all bank accounts, and investments, The blessings of the Lord overtake me in every area of my life and I do receive them (Deut. 28:1-14).*

*I decree that I am like a tree planted by rivers of water, I bring forth fruit in my*

*season; my leaf shall not wither and what-
ever I do will prosper (Psalm 1:3).*

*I decree that God has opened unto me
His good treasure and He has blessed the
work of my hands (Deut. 28:8).*

*I decree that I meditate on the Word
day and night and obey the Word and my
business is prospering and I will have good
success (Joshua 1:8).*

*I decree that grace and peace be multi-
plied to me as I manage my business (2 Peter
1:2).*

## YOUR CITY/ NATION

*Father, according to you Word, I declare
that blessed is (your city/nation) whose God
is the Lord (Psalms 33:12).*

*I decree that the leaders of this nation
trust in the Lord and lean not to their
own understanding, in all their ways they
acknowledge Him they He may direct their
paths. (Proverbs 3:5).*

*I decree an awakening in America.
Awake America and put on your strength in
the Lord! (Isaiah 51:9).*

*I decree that God is turning the heart of America back to Him and I decree that the Kingdom of God is advancing on earth in America as it is in heaven (Malachi 4:6, Matthew 6:10).*

*Father your Word declares that righteousness exalts a nation: but sin is a reproach to any people. I decree that righteousness prevails in America (Proverbs 13:34).*

*Father your Word declares, that the fear of the LORD is the beginning of wisdom: and the knowledge of the holy is understanding. I decree that a Holy Fear has come upon America and she shall walk in God's wisdom and understanding (Proverbs 9:10).*

*I decree peace to come to Jerusalem in the Name of Yeshua (Psalms 122:6).*

Made in the USA
San Bernardino, CA
26 February 2017